M000278087

Earth Systems

elevate science
MODULES

SAVVAS
LEARNING COMPANY

AUTHORS

You're an author!

As you write in this science book, your answers and personal discoveries will be recorded for you to keep, making this book unique to you. That is why you are one of the primary authors of this book.

✏️ In the space below, print your name, school, town, and state. Then write a short autobiography that includes your interests and accomplishments.

YOUR NAME _Macy Muir_

SCHOOL _Friday harbor middle school_

TOWN, STATE _San Juan Island_

AUTOBIOGRAPHY _____

_____

Your Photo

The cover photo shows Havasu Falls.

Front cover: Waterfall, Lightphoto/iStock/Getty Images; Back cover: Science Doodle, LHF Graphics/Shutterstock.

LEARNING COMPANY

ISBN-13:   978-1-418-29160-0
ISBN-10:   1-418-29160-9
6   21

Program Authors

ZIPPORAH MILLER, Ed.D.
Coordinator for K-12 Science Programs, Anne Arundel County Public Schools
Dr. Zipporah Miller currently serves as the Senior Manager for Organizational Learning with the Anne Arundel County Public School System. Prior to that she served as the K-12 Coordinator for science in Anne Arundel County. She conducts national training to science stakeholders on the Next Generation Science Standards. Dr. Miller also served as the Associate Executive Director for Professional Development Programs and conferences at the National Science Teachers Association (NSTA) and served as a reviewer during the development of Next Generation Science Standards. Dr. Miller holds a doctoral degree from the University of Maryland College Park, a master's degree in school administration and supervision from Bowie State University and a bachelor's degree from Chadron State College.

MICHAEL J. PADILLA, Ph.D.
Professor Emeritus, Eugene P. Moore School of Education, Clemson University, Clemson, South Carolina
Michael J. Padilla taught science in middle and secondary schools, has more than 30 years of experience educating middle-school science teachers, and served as one of the writers of the 1996 U.S. National Science Education Standards. In recent years Mike has focused on teaching science to English Language Learners. His extensive experience as Principal Investigator on numerous National Science Foundation and U.S. Department of Education grants resulted in more than $35 million in funding to improve science education. He served as president of the National Science Teachers Association, the world's largest science teaching organization, in 2005–6.

MICHAEL E. WYSESSION, Ph.D
Professor of Earth and Planetary Sciences, Washington University, St. Louis, Missouri
Author of more than 100 science and science education publications, Dr. Wysession was awarded the prestigious National Science Foundation Presidential Faculty Fellowship and Packard Foundation Fellowship for his research in geophysics, primarily focused on using seismic tomography to determine the forces driving plate tectonics. Dr. Wysession is also a leader in geoscience literacy and education; he is the chair of the Earth Science Literacy Initiative, the author of several popular video lectures on geology in the *Great Courses* series, and a lead writer of the *Next Generation Science Standards**.

REVIEWERS

Program Consultants

Carol Baker
Science Curriculum

Dr. Carol K. Baker is superintendent for Lyons Elementary K-8 School District in Lyons, Illinois. Prior to this, she was Director of Curriculum for Science and Music in Oak Lawn, Illinois. Before this she taught Physics and Earth Science for 18 years. In the recent past, Dr. Baker also wrote assessment questions for ACT (EXPLORE and PLAN), was elected president of the Illinois Science Teachers Association from 2011–2013, and served as a member of the Museum of Science and Industry (Chicago) advisory board. She is a writer of the Next Generation Science Standards. Dr. Baker received her B.S. in Physics and a science teaching certification. She completed her master's of Educational Administration (K-12) and earned her doctorate in Educational Leadership.

Jim Cummins
ELL

Dr. Cummins's research focuses on literacy development in multilingual schools and the role technology plays in learning across the curriculum. *Elevate Science* incorporates research-based principles for integrating language with the teaching of academic content based on Dr. Cummins's work.

Elfrieda Hiebert
Literacy

Dr. Hiebert, a former primary-school teacher, is President and CEO of TextProject, a non-profit aimed at providing open-access resources for instruction of beginning and struggling readers, She is also a research associate at the University of California Santa Cruz. Her research addresses how fluency, vocabulary, and knowledge can be fostered through appropriate texts, and her contributions have been recognized through awards such as the Oscar Causey Award for Outstanding Contributions to Reading Research (Literacy Research Association, 2015), Research to Practice award (American Educational Research Association, 2013), and the William S. Gray Citation of Merit Award for Outstanding Contributions to Reading Research (International Reading Association, 2008).

Content Reviewers

Alex Blom, Ph.D.
Associate Professor
Department Of Physical Sciences
Alverno College
Milwaukee, Wisconsin

Joy Branlund, Ph.D.
Department of Physical Science
Southwestern Illinois College
Granite City, Illinois

Judy Calhoun
Associate Professor
Physical Sciences
Alverno College
Milwaukee, Wisconsin

Stefan Debbert
Associate Professor of Chemistry
Lawrence University
Appleton, Wisconsin

Diane Doser
Professor
Department of Geological Sciences
University of Texas at El Paso
El Paso, Texas

Rick Duhrkopf, Ph.D.
Department of Biology
Baylor University
Waco, Texas

Jennifer Liang
University of Minnesota Duluth
Duluth, Minnesota

Heather Mernitz, Ph.D.
Associate Professor of Physical
 Sciences
Alverno College
Milwaukee, Wisconsin

Joseph McCullough, Ph.D.
Cabrillo College
Aptos, California

Katie M. Nemeth, Ph.D.
Assistant Professor
College of Science and Engineering
University of Minnesota Duluth
Duluth, Minnesota

Maik Pertermann
Department of Geology
Western Wyoming Community College
Rock Springs, Wyoming

Scott Rochette
Department of the Earth Sciences
The College at Brockport
 State University of New York
Brockport, New York

David Schuster
Washington University in St Louis
St. Louis, Missouri

Shannon Stevenson
Department of Biology
University of Minnesota Duluth
Duluth, Minnesota

Paul Stoddard, Ph.D.
Department of Geology and
 Environmental Geosciences
Northern Illinois University
DeKalb, Illinois

Nancy Taylor
American Public University
Charles Town, West Virginia

Teacher Reviewers

Jennifer Bennett, M.A.
Memorial Middle School
Tampa, Florida

Sonia Blackstone
Lake County Schools
Howey In the Hills, Florida

Teresa Bode
Roosevelt Elementary
Tampa, Florida

Tyler C. Britt, Ed.S.
Curriculum & Instructional
Practice Coordinator
Raytown Quality Schools
Raytown, Missouri

A. Colleen Campos
Grandview High School
Aurora, Colorado

Ronald Davis
Riverview Elementary
Riverview, Florida

Coleen Doulk
Challenger School
Spring Hill, Florida

Mary D. Dube
Burnett Middle School
Seffner, Florida

Sandra Galpin
Adams Middle School
Tampa, Florida

Margaret Henry
Lebanon Junior High School
Lebanon, Ohio

Christina Hill
Beth Shields Middle School
Ruskin, Florida

Judy Johnis
Gorden Burnett Middle School
Seffner, Florida

Karen Y. Johnson
Beth Shields Middle School
Ruskin, Florida

Jane Kemp
Lockhart Elementary School
Tampa, Florida

Denise Kuhling
Adams Middle School
Tampa, Florida

Esther Leonard, M.Ed. and L.M.T.
Gifted and talented Implementation Specialist
San Antonio Independent School District
San Antonio, Texas

Kelly Maharaj
Challenger K–8 School of Science
and Mathematics
Spring Hill, Florida

Kevin J. Maser, Ed.D.
H. Frank Carey Jr/Sr High School
Franklin Square, New York

Angie L. Matamoros, Ph.D.
ALM Science Consultant
Weston, Florida

Corey Mayle
Brogden Middle School
Durham, North Carolina

Keith McCarthy
George Washington Middle School
Wayne, New Jersey

Yolanda O. Peña
John F. Kennedy Junior High School
West Valley City, Utah

Kathleen M. Poe
Jacksonville Beach Elementary School
Jacksonville Beach, Florida

Wendy Rauld
Monroe Middle School
Tampa, Florida

Anne Rice
Woodland Middle School
Gurnee, Illinois

Bryna Selig
Gaithersburg Middle School
Gaithersburg, Maryland

Pat (Patricia) Shane, Ph.D.
STEM & ELA Education Consultant
Chapel Hill, North Carolina

Diana Shelton
Burnett Middle School
Seffner, Florida

Nakia Sturrup
Jennings Middle School
Seffner, Florida

Melissa Triebwasser
Walden Lake Elementary
Plant City, Florida

Michele Bubley Wiehagen
Science Coach
Miles Elementary School
Tampa, Florida

Pauline Wilcox
Instructional Science Coach
Fox Chapel Middle School
Spring Hill, Florida

Safety Reviewers

Douglas Mandt, M.S.
Science Education Consultant
Edgewood, Washington

Juliana Textley, Ph.D.
Author, NSTA books on school science safety
Adjunct Professor
Lesley University
Cambridge, Massachusetts

Go to SavvasRealize.com to access your digital course.

VIDEO
• Aquaculture Manager

INTERACTIVITY
• Describing Systems
• Thermal Energy and the Cycling of Matter
• Maps and Methods
• Constructive and Destructive Forces
• The Water Cycle
• Siting a Fish Farm
• Floridan Aquifer System

VIRTUAL LAB
• Changes in the Water Cycle

ASSESSMENT

eTEXT

HANDS-ON LABS

иConnect What Interactions Occur Within the Earth System?

иInvestigate
• Where Heat Flows
• Surface Features
• Water on Earth

иDemonstrate
Modeling a Watershed

TOPIC 2

Minerals and Rocks in the Geosphere 44

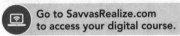

Go to SavvasRealize.com
to access your digital course.

▶ **VIDEO**
• Product Engineer

👆 **INTERACTIVITY**
• Hot on the Inside
• Earth's Layers
• Comparing Earth and the Moon
• Designing Satellites
• So Many, Many Minerals
• Mineral Management
• Don't Take it for Granite
• Is There a Geologist in the House?
• Rocky Changes
• Rock Cycle
• Rocks on the Move

📱 **VIRTUAL LAB**
• Rocks and Minerals: The Story of Earth

☑ **ASSESSMENT**

📖 **eTEXT**

HANDS-ON LABS

uConnect Build a Model of Earth

uInvestigate
• Heat and Motion in a Liquid
• Mineral Mash-Up
• Growing a Crystal Garden
• A Sequined Rock
• Ages of Rocks

uDemonstrate
The Rock Cycle in Action

TOPIC

3

Plate Tectonics 94

The Essential Question How do geological processes change Earth's surface?

Quest KICKOFF To Hike or Not to Hike 96

иConnect Lab How Are Earth's Continents
Linked Together? 97A

MS-ESS2-2, MS-ESS2-3, MS-ESS3-2

Go to SavvasRealize.com
to access your digital course.

▶ **VIDEO**
- Volcanologist

👆 **INTERACTIVITY**
- Land and Seafloor Patterns
- Slow and Steady
- By No Fault of Their Own
- Relative Plate Motion
- Stressed to a Fault
- Earthquake Engineering
- Locating an Earthquake
- Placing a Bay Area Stadium
- Landforms from Volcanic Activity
- Volcanoes Changing Earth's Surface

📱 **VIRTUAL LAB**
- Geological Processes and Evil Plans

☑ **ASSESSMENT**

📖 **eTEXT**

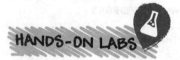

HANDS-ON LABS

иConnect How Are Earth's Continents
Linked Together?

иInvestigate
- Piecing Together a Supercontinent
- Plate Interactions
- Analyze Earthquake Data to Identify
  Patterns
- Moving Volcanoes

иDemonstrate
Model Sea-Floor Spreading

Go to SavvasRealize.com to access your digital course.

▶ VIDEO
• Paleontologist

👆 INTERACTIVITY
• Oldest to Youngest
• Radiometric Dating
• Know Your Index Fossils
• On the Clock
• A Very Grand Canyon
• Going Away
• How Old Are These Rocks?
• Observation and Deduction
• Big Changes

🧪 VIRTUAL LAB
• The Story in the Strata

☑ ASSESSMENT

📖 eTEXT

HANDS-ON LABS

иConnect Dividing History

иInvestigate
• The Story in Rocks
• Going Back in Time
• Changes in the Water

иDemonstrate
Core Sampling Through Time

ix

Elevate your thinking!

Elevate Science takes science to a whole new level and lets you take ownership of your learning. Explore science in the world around you. Investigate how things work. Think critically and solve problems! *Elevate Science* helps you think like a scientist, so you're ready for a world of discoveries.

Explore Your World

Explore real-life scenarios with engaging Quests that dig into science topics around the world. You can:

- Solve real-world problems
- Apply skills and knowledge
- Communicate solutions

Make Connections

Elevate Science connects science to other subjects and shows you how to better understand the world through:

- Mathematics
- Reading and Writing
- Literacy

Quest KICKOFF

What do you think is causing Pleasant Pond to turn green?

In 2016, algal blooms turned bodies of water green and slimy in Florida, Utah, California, and 17 other states. These blooms put people and ecosystems in danger. Scientists, such as limnologists, are working to predict and prevent future algal blooms. In this problem-based Quest activity, you will investigate an algal bloom at a lake and determine its cause. In labs and digital activities, you will apply what you learn in each lesson to help you gather evidence to solve the mystery. With enough evidence, you will be able to identify what you believe is the cause of the algal bloom and present a solution in the Findings activity.

Math Toolbox

Graphing Population Changes

Ohio's Deer Population

Changes in a population over time, such as white-tailed deer in Ohio, can be displayed in a graph.

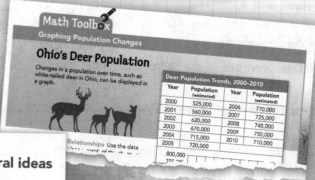

Deer Population Trends, 2000–2010

Year	Population (estimated)	Year	Population (estimated)
2000	525,000	2006	770,000
2001	560,000	2007	725,000
2002	620,000	2008	745,000
2003	670,000	2009	750,000
2004	715,000	2010	710,000
2005	720,000		

Relationships Use the data

800,000
750,000

READING CHECK **Determine Central Ideas**
What adaptations might the giraffe have that help it survive in its environment?

Academic Vocabulary

Relate the term *decomposer* to the verb *compose*. What does it mean to compose something?

Build Skills for the Future

- Master the Engineering Design Process
- Apply critical thinking and analytical skills
- Learn about STEM careers

Focus on Inquiry

Case studies put you in the shoes of a scientist to solve real-world mysteries using real data. You will be able to:

- Analyze Data
- Test a hypothesis
- Solve the Case

Case Study

MS-LS2-1

THE CASE OF THE DISAPPEARING

Cerulean Warbler

The cerulean warbler is a small, migratory songbird named for its blue color. Cerulean warblers breed in eastern North America during the spring and summer. The warblers spend the winter months in the Andes Mountains of Colombia, Venezuela, Ecuador, and Peru in northern part of South America.

Enter the Lab

Hands-on experiments and virtual labs help you test ideas and show what you know in performance-based assessments. Scaffolded labs include:

- STEM Labs
- Design Your Own
- Open-ended Labs

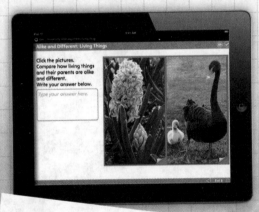

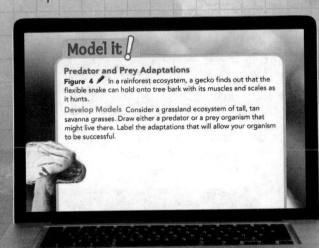

HANDS-ON LAB

Investigate Observe how once-living matter is broken down into smaller components in the process of decomposition.

TOPIC

1

Introduction to Earth's Systems

NGSS PERFORMANCE EXPECTATIONS

MS-ESS2-1 Develop a model to describe the cycling of Earth's materials and the flow of energy that drives this process.

MS-ESS2-4 Develop a model to describe the cycling of water through Earth's systems driven by energy from the sun and the force of gravity.

HANDS-ON LAB

uConnect Develop a model to describe interactions among Earth's spheres.

GO ONLINE
to access your
digital course

 VIDEO

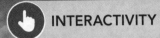 INTERACTIVITY

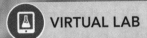 VIRTUAL LAB

 ASSESSMENT

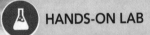 eTEXT

HANDS-ON LAB

How do all the things
in this photo interact
with each other?

The Essential Question

How do matter and energy cycle through Earth's systems?

CCC Systems and System Models How do water, rock, air, and
organisms interact to make Earth's surface features and systems?

....

....

....

....

....

....

....

Quest KICKOFF

How can you predict the effects of a forest fire?

Phenomenon You just watched a news report about a wildfire that is burning just north of your town. The fire is not under control, and you wonder what will happen to the forest. In this problem-based Quest activity, you will take on the role of a scientist whose task is to educate and inform local residents about the harmful effects of a forest fire. You will consider how all the spheres of the Earth system interact, then use that information to make predictions about the outcome of the fire's damage. Your presentation will take the form of a poster, photo essay, or a multimedia report.

 INTERACTIVITY

Forest Fires

MS-ESS2-1 Develop a model to describe the cycling of Earth's materials and the flow of energy that drives this process.
MS-ESS2-4 Develop a model to describe the cycling of water through Earth's systems driven by energy from the sun and the force of gravity.

NBC LEARN ▶ VIDEO

After watching the Quest Kickoff video, which explores the effects of a forest fire, record ways in which a fire will impact Earth's spheres.

Organisms:

....

....

Ground/Earth:

....

....

Air:

....

....

Water:

....

....

Quest CHECK-IN

IN LESSON 1

How can an event in one sphere, such as the atmosphere, have an impact on another sphere? Think about the flow of energy as the fire started, then spread.

 INTERACTIVITY

Fire and Earth's Spheres

Quest CHECK-IN

IN LESSON 2

How do all of Earth's spheres interact? Consider these interactions as you learn how fire affects the geosphere.

 INTERACTIVITY

Disrupting the Geosphere

Fires are part of the natural life cycle of a forest. However, when they happen at the wrong time or burn for too long, forest fires have a devastating effect on plant and animal populations. Fires also affect the surrounding air, water, and land.

Quest CHECK-IN

IN LESSON 3

How does the hydrosphere interact with the other spheres, and vice versa? Examine the effects of fire on the hydrosphere. Then review all data and finalize your predictions.

👆 **INTERACTIVITY**

Impact on the Hydrosphere

Quest FINDINGS

Complete the Quest!

Create an engaging presentation to summarize your findings. Reflect on how the spheres influence each other—and your town.

👆 **INTERACTIVITY**

Reflect on Forest Fires

What Interactions Occur Within the Earth System?

How can you **develop and use a model** to describe interactions within the Earth system?

Background

Phenomenon You read in an article that "Scientists classify matter on Earth into four spheres: living things, rocks, water, and air. The spheres interact and form the Earth system." You wonder how the spheres interact. You turn the page, only to find the rest of the article is missing. When you ask your teacher to help you understand the Earth system, he challenges you to complete the article by doing your own analysis of interactions among Earth's spheres.

Materials

(per group)

- index cards in green, yellow, blue, and white
- bulletin board
- pushpins
- poster paper
- variety of art and office supplies, such as the following: tape, markers, colored paper, scissors, paper cups, yarn or string, magazines, newspapers, staples, and stapler

Develop a Model

1. Get an index card from your teacher. Join other students with the same color card to form a sphere group. Green is living things, yellow is rocks, blue is water, and white is air.

2. As a group, brainstorm about matter that makes up your sphere. Discuss these questions. Record your ideas in the table.
   - What are some of properties, or characteristics of the matter in your sphere?
   - What are some examples of living things/rocks/water/air in your town, state, or elsewhere? How do they change or move?

3. Read the number on your card. Join other students with the same number to form an Earth system group.

4. Share what you know about your sphere with your group. Then brainstorm how different spheres interact with and affect each other. Discuss these questions. Record your ideas in the table.
   - In what ways does your sphere depend on other spheres?
   - How do parts of your sphere move within or cycle through other spheres?

Be sure to follow all safety procedures provided by your teacher. The Safety Appendix of your textbook provides more details about the safety icons.

5. **SEP Develop a Model** As a group, build an Earth system model that illustrates the interactions among the spheres. Include specific examples.

HANDS-ON LAB

uConnect Go online for a downloadable worksheet of this lab.

Observations

Ideas About Your Sphere	Ideas About Sphere Interactions

Analyze and Conclude

1. **SEP Use a Model** How did you represent Earth's spheres and the interactions between those spheres in your model?

....
....
....
....

2. **CCC Energy and Matter** How might matter represented in your model move from one sphere to another on Earth? Give two examples.

....
....

3. **SEP Communicate Scientific Information** Complete the magazine article by writing a paragraph that describes at least three interactions between Earth's spheres.

....
....
....

① Matter and Energy in Earth's System

Guiding Questions

- What are the different components of the Earth system?
- What are the sources of energy for the processes that affect Earth?
- How can you model the cycling of matter in the Earth system?

Connections

Literacy Cite Textual Evidence

Math Interpret a Line Graph

MS-ESS2-1

HANDS-ON LAB

uInvestigate Model how energy flows within Earth.

Vocabulary

atmosphere
geosphere
hydrosphere
cryosphere
biosphere
energy

Academic Vocabulary

system
feedback

Connect It !

✎ **Draw a line on the photo to indicate where the surface of the lake was in the past.**

CCC Cause and Effect What happened to the water in this lake? Why do you think this happened?

....

....

The Earth System

Lake Mead, shown in **Figure 1**, is part of a large system consisting of the Colorado River, Hoover Dam, and Las Vegas, Nevada. A **system** is a group of parts that work together as a whole. If we zoom way out, the universe is the biggest system of all, and it contains all other systems. Earth is a system, too.

Water and Rock Cycles The Earth system involves flows of matter and energy through different components. In the water cycle, water evaporates from the ocean and other bodies of water. Then it rises into the atmosphere and eventually falls back to Earth's surface as precipitation. Rain and meltwater then flow to rivers, lakes, and the ocean. Eventually the water cycles back into the atmosphere. At each step of a cycle of matter, some change in energy occurs to keep the cycle going. Evaporation of water requires heat energy. The heat energy may come from the sun or from within Earth, as in a hot spring.

Rock also cycles through the Earth system. Hot molten material inside Earth, called magma, flows up through cracks in Earth's crust. This new material cools—loses heat energy—to form solid rock. Over time, the rock can be eroded into small pieces. If enough small pieces collect, they may get packed together to form new rock.

☑ READING CHECK **Compare and Contrast** How are the rock and water cycles similar? How are they different?

....

....

....

....

👆 **INTERACTIVITY**

Explore different types of systems.

Academic Vocabulary

Much of science involves identifying components of different systems. List two systems you hear about in everyday life. What are their components?

....

....

....

....

....

....

....

The Cycling of Water
Figure 1 Drought has had a serious impact on Lake Mead, a reservoir in Nevada.

VIDEO

Learn about the main spheres of Earth's system and how they interact.

Literacy Connection

Cite Textual Evidence
Reread the sections about the atmosphere. Underline the evidence that supports the idea that the atmosphere affects Earth's climate.

Earth's Spheres The Earth system is made up of four main spheres, or subsystems, shown in **Figure 2**. Earth's **atmosphere** (AT muh sfeer) is the relatively thin envelope of gases that forms Earth's outermost layer. It is made of air—a mixture of gases including nitrogen, oxygen, water vapor, and carbon dioxide—and dust particles. It contains Earth's weather, and it is the foundation for the different climates around the world. Most of Earth's mass is in the form of rock and metal of the **geosphere** (GEE uh sfeer). The geosphere includes the solid metal inner core, the liquid metal outer core, and the rocky mantle and crust. All of Earth's water, including water that cycles through the atmosphere, is called the **hydrosphere** (HI druh sfeer). The **cryosphere** (CRY uh sfeer) is the frozen component of the hydrosphere. It is made up of all the ice and snow on land, plus sea and lake ice. The parts of Earth that contain all living organisms are collectively known as the **biosphere** (BI uh sfeer).

Earth's outermost layer receives energy in the form of sunlight that passes through it and from heat that rises from Earth's surface, including the ocean. Heat rising from Earth's surface creates wind, which distributes heat as well as water through the atmosphere.

Earth's rock and metal contain an enormous amount of energy. Exposed rock absorbs sunlight and radiates heat into the atmosphere. In some locations, energy and new material make up the rocky outer layer of the geosphere in the form of lava. Major eruptions can affect the atmosphere, which in turn affects the hydrosphere and biosphere.

Energy Flow The constant flow, or cycling, of matter through the Earth system requires energy. **Energy** is the ability to do work. The Earth system has two main sources of energy: heat from the sun and heat from Earth's interior. These energy sources drive cycles of matter in the four spheres.

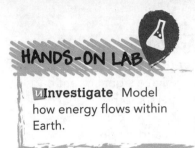

HANDS-ON LAB

Investigate Model how energy flows within Earth.

✓ READING CHECK **Use Information** Which part of each sphere do you interact with in your daily life? Give one example for each of the main spheres.

....

....

....

Earth's Spheres

Figure 2 Earth has four major spheres that cycle matter and energy and shape Earth's surface. Label each box with the correct sphere name. Then, list at least two spheres that show an interaction within the photo.

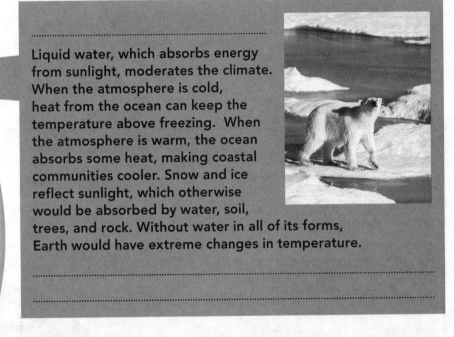

Liquid water, which absorbs energy from sunlight, moderates the climate. When the atmosphere is cold, heat from the ocean can keep the temperature above freezing. When the atmosphere is warm, the ocean absorbs some heat, making coastal communities cooler. Snow and ice reflect sunlight, which otherwise would be absorbed by water, soil, trees, and rock. Without water in all of its forms, Earth would have extreme changes in temperature.

Life has been found in virtually every part of Earth, from deep below the continental ice shelf of Antarctica to high up in the Himalayan Mountains.

Feedback involves a loop in which a signal or action triggers another signal or action. This can happen when a microphone picks up sound from a speaker that is amplifying the microphone's signal. The equipment passes the signal back and forth, and it becomes louder and harsher. What is one form of feedback that you encounter in your life?

....

....

....

....

System Feedback

Glaciers, part of the cryosphere, are large blocks of ancient ice, usually found near mountains and in polar regions. Like a freezer pack in a cooler, a glacier keeps the surrounding air and land cool. But many glaciers are melting around the world. As glaciers melt, they lose mass and volume and turn into liquid water that drains away or evaporates. This allows the land underneath to absorb more sunlight, which causes the surrounding air and land to get warmer. The warmer air makes glaciers melt even faster. This is an example of **feedback**. The system returns, or feeds back, information about itself, and that information results in change.

Positive and Negative Feedback
Sometimes feedback is negative: it causes a process to slow down, or go in reverse. But some types of feedback are positive: they reinforce, speed up, or enhance the process that's already underway. Feedback may result in stability or it may cause more change. The melting glaciers are an example of positive feedback and change. A similar process is causing change in the Arctic.

☑ READING CHECK **Cite Textual Evidence** Name a reason why melting glaciers are considered positive feedback.

....

....

Model It!

Sea Ice and Climate
Figure 3 Liquid and solid water are important factors in controlling climate. A large body of water can absorb energy from the sun, while snow or ice reflects solar energy back into space. In recent years, the amount of sea ice—frozen water—in the Arctic Circle has been dwindling because the air and water have been warmer than usual. As more of the Arctic Ocean is exposed due to loss of ice, it absorbs more sunlight and gets warmer. This makes it less likely for sea ice to form even when the air is well below freezing.

CCC Energy and Matter 🖉 On the image provided, draw and label a cycle diagram for the feedback that is occurring in the Arctic among ice, liquid seawater, atmosphere, and solar energy.

Sea Ice

Arcticc Sea Ice

Historically, Arctic winters had long, dark nights and seawater froze. In the warmer summers, much of the sea ice melted. Today, more Arctic ice melts in summer than it has in human history. The total area of Arctic sea ice has changed in recent years as the globe has warmed. The graph shows the amount of sea ice found in the Arctic Ocean for the following years: 1986, 1996, 2006, and 2016.

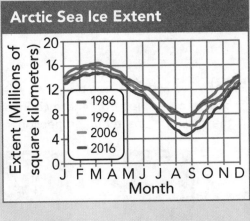

Arctic Sea Ice Extent

1. **CCC Patterns** What is the trend in the data?

....

2. **Interpret a Line Graph** What was the lowest extent of sea ice in the data, and when did it occur?

....

3. **CCC Stability and Change** What will happen to the extent of sea ice in the Arctic if temperatures continue to rise? Incorporate what you know about "feedback" into your prediction.

....
....
....

Interacting Spheres An event in one sphere can affect another, which in turn can affect another. For example, Greenland is losing about 250 billion tons of ice each year. As the massive ice sheet thins, the weight of the ice decreases. As a result, in some parts of Greenland, the land is rising about 1.0 cm per year. How can this happen? Earth's rocky outer layer is floating on a denser layer of rock below the crust.

A landmass that gets heavier by gaining more water or other material will "sink," while a landmass that gets lighter by losing material will rise. It's like a boat in the water with its cargo off-loaded, as shown in **Figure 4**. As containers are removed, there's less mass on the boat. This causes the boat to sit higher in the water because it is more buoyant.

INTERACTIVITY

Examine thermal energy and the cycling of matter in Earth's spheres.

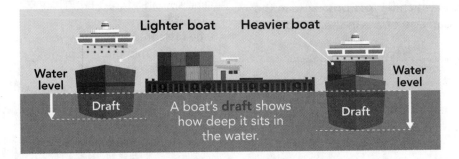

Buoyancy of Landmasses

Figure 4 A landmass can rise and sit higher on Earth's surface if it sheds a lot of mass, just like a boat floating on water.

☑ LESSON 1 Check

MS-ESS2-1

1. Identify What is the term for the part of the hydrosphere that is frozen?

....

2. SEP Use Models Use the rock cycle diagram below to describe how energy is involved in the cycling of matter in the geosphere.

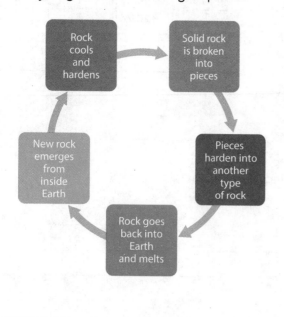

....
....
....
....

3. CCC Cause and Effect During the water cycle, water evaporates, rises into the atmosphere, and eventually falls back to Earth's surface as precipitation. What is the original source of energy that produces these changes?

....
....
....
....

4. CCC Systems Give an example of the hydrosphere interacting with the geosphere.

....
....
....
....
....

5. Connect to the Environment Give an example of how changes in the cryosphere affect the biosphere.

....
....
....
....
....

Quest CHECK-IN

In this lesson, you learned about the different spheres that make up Earth. You also learned how these spheres affect and shape each other, and how feedback within or between spheres produces stability or change.

Evaluate What are three ways in which factors or events in the atmosphere could increase the damage of fire in the biosphere?

....
....
....
....

 **INTERACTIVITY**

Fire and Earth's Spheres

Go online to trace how the forest fire started and discover factors that can start and spread a forest fire. Think about the flow of energy as the fire spreads and how you might use this information in your presentation.

10   Introduction to Earth's Systems

MS-ESS2-1, MS-ESS2-4

When the ICE MELTS

Florida, a semi-tropical paradise far from the northern latitudes, might seem to have nothing to do with Greenland, the island of ice between the Atlantic and Arctic Oceans. But Florida is a coastal state with one of the largest populations in the United States.

And if you live near the coast, then you'll definitely want to pay attention to what's happening in Greenland. About 82 percent of Greenland is covered by an ice sheet. But in recent years, this ice sheet has been melting at an advanced rate due to warming global temperatures. When ice on land melts and runs into the ocean, it has the potential to raise sea levels around the world.

Sea levels have risen at an average rate of 1.5 cm every decade for the last century. But during the last 25 years, that rate has doubled, mostly as a result of ice melting in Greenland and Antarctica.

Higher sea levels threaten infrastructure, such as roadways or utility lines, as well as lives and property. The higher the sea level, the more vulnerable Florida is to deadly storms and coastal flooding. Government officials and scientists from a variety of fields are working together to create and implement protection measures to deal with potential problems in the future.

MY COMMUNITY

How would you deal with the problem of rising sea levels? Go online to research what Florida or another coastal state is doing to protect its coastline from the encroaching ocean.

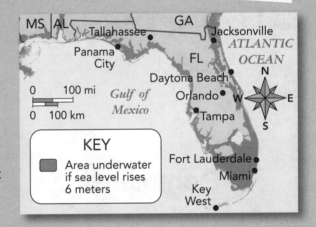

If the entire ice sheet on Greenland melted, sea levels would rise about 7 meters.

Surface Features in the Geosphere

Guiding Questions

- What are the different landforms found on Earth?
- What forces and energy make the different landforms?
- What are the various ways to model landforms?

Connections

Literacy Write Explanatory Texts

Math Analyze Quantitative Relationships

MS-ESS2-1

HANDS-ON LAB

uInvestigate Model landforms to learn about elevation and relief.

Vocabulary
topography
landform
mountain
coastline
dune
river
delta
surveying

Academic Vocabulary
model

Connect It !

✏️ **Circle the places of high elevation in the Western and Eastern United States. What other features do you notice on the map?**

SEP Make Observations What observations can you make about the elevations of the coasts and center of the United States?

....

....

SEP Apply Scientific Reasoning Do you think other countries around the world also have a variety of land elevations? Explain.

....

....

Topography of the Geosphere

If you drove across the United States, you would observe many changes in topography, as shown in **Figure 1**. **Topography** (tuh PAWG ruh fee) is the shape of the land. Land can be described using elevation, relief, and landforms.

The height of a point above sea level on Earth's surface is its elevation. California has the lowest and highest points of elevation in the contiguous United States. The lowest point, found at Badwater Basin in Death Valley, is 86 meters below sea level. The highest elevation is Mount Whitney at 4,418 meters. The difference in elevation between the highest and lowest points of an area is its relief. An area's relief is the result of the different landforms found there. **Landforms** are features such as coastlines, dunes, and mountains. Different landforms have different combinations of elevation and relief.

✅ **READING CHECK** **Determine Central Ideas** Explain the three ways that land can be described.

....

....

....

....

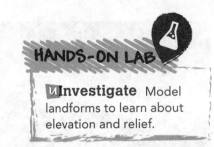

HANDS-ON LAB

u**Investigate** Model landforms to learn about elevation and relief.

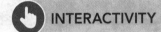

INTERACTIVITY

Think about landforms that can be found in Florida.

Relief Map

Figure 1 The United States has many different land features such as mountains, rivers, and plains.

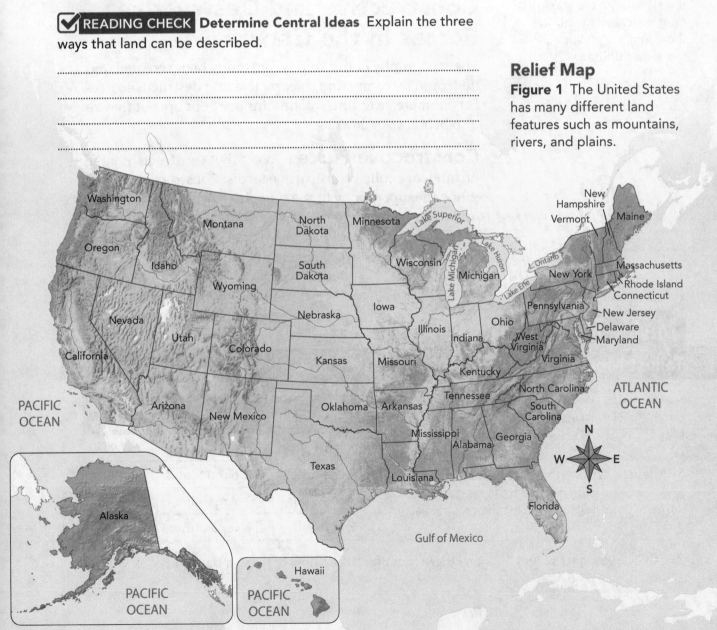

13

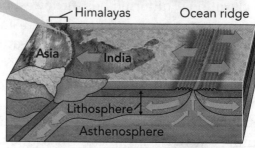

Ocean ridge

Asia

India

Lithosphere

Asthenosphere

Himalayas

Ocean ridge

Asia

India

Lithosphere

Asthenosphere

← N

Plates Collide

Figure 2 India was pushed against Asia, which caused the formation of the Himalayan mountain range, located mainly in the countries of Nepal, India, and Bhutan.

Constructive and Destructive Forces in the Geosphere

The topography of the land is constantly being created and destroyed by competing constructive and destructive forces. For example, over time, mountains are built up, but they're also being worn down.

Constructive Forces Forces that construct, or build up land, are called constructive forces. Constructive forces shape the topography in the geosphere by creating mountains and other huge landmasses. The Himalayan mountain range in Asia formed over millions of years, as India collided with Asia and pushed up sections of the ocean floor, as shown in **Figure 2**.

 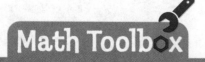

Math Toolbox

Tallest Mountains

As the plates continue to push against each other, the Himalayas are still rising to new heights. Mount Everest is the world's tallest mountain.

Mountain	Location	Height (meters)
Kilimanjaro	Tanzania	5,895
Denali	United States	6,190
Aconcagua	Argentina	6,962
Everest	Nepal/Tibet	8,850

1. **Analyze Quantitative Relationships** According to the data from the table, about how many times taller is Everest than Kilimanjaro?

....

2. **CCC Cause and Effect** What might account for the heights of these mountains?

....

A volcano erupts.

....

The eruption sends ash and gases into the air.

....

Lava and ash flow down into the surrounding habitats.

....

Mudflows form when ash and other volcanic material mix with water.

....

Destructive Forces The Himalayas were formed because land was built up, but there are destructive forces that also change Earth's topography. For example, rain, wind, ice, and fire destroy and wear away landmasses and affect the geosphere.

The geosphere, atmosphere, hydrosphere, and biosphere interact with each other to affect Earth. For example, an event that occurs in the geosphere, such as the volcano in **Figure 3**, will change the other spheres. A volcano releases ash and gases into the atmosphere and volcanic material into the hydrosphere. Initially, the volcanic material and gases may kill organisms in the biosphere. However, ash can enrich the soil and give new plants more nutrients. Hardened lava may cut off old river channels but form a new lake.

✓ READING CHECK **Integrate With Visuals** Refer to the art in **Figure 2** that shows the collision of India with Asia. How did changes in the geosphere cause the Himalayas to form?

....

....

A Volcano Changes Everything
Figure 3 🖉 A volcano causes changes in four spheres. Record which sphere is affected during each step in an eruption.

Literacy Connection

Write Explanatory Texts As you read, number the steps in which an erupting volcano starts the cycle of change. Then, think about a forest fire. Explain how a fire would affect the geosphere, atmosphere, hydrosphere, and biosphere.

Exploring Earth's Surface

There are a variety of landforms on Earth because Earth's surface differs from place to place. In addition, landforms change over time due to constructive and destructive forces. Some landforms are snow-capped mountains, some are giant glaciers, and others are ever-changing sand dunes. **Figure 4** shows some of the landforms found on Earth.

Many Landforms

Figure 4 🖉 There are so many different landforms, but they are all connected. Choose two landforms. Draw a line from one landform to another and tell how they are connected to each other.

....

....

....

....

Mountains

A **mountain** is a landform with both high elevation and high relief. Mountains that are closely related in shape, structure, location, and age are called a mountain range. Different mountain ranges in one region make up a mountain system. The Rocky Mountains are a famous mountain system. Mountain ranges and mountain systems in a long, connected chain form a larger unit called a mountain belt.

Plateaus and Plains

Landforms that have high elevation and low relief are called plateaus. Streams and rivers may cut into the plateau's surface. Landforms that have low elevation and low relief are called plains. A plain that lies along a seacoast is called a coastal plain. In North America, the Atlantic coastal plain extends from Florida all the way up to Cape Cod in Massachusetts.

Plateau

Lake

Plain

Dune

Coastlines The boundary between the land and the ocean or a lake is the **coastline**. Among the 50 states, the mainland of Alaska has the longest coastline at 10,686 kilometers. The mainland of Florida has the second longest coastline, measuring 2,170 kilometers.

Dunes The land that extends from a coastline may be rocky cliffs, sandy beaches, or dunes. A **dune** is a hill of sand piled up by the wind. Dunes in the coastal regions are parallel to the coastline and protect the land from ocean waves.

Rivers and Deltas A **river** is a natural stream of water that flows into another body of water such as an ocean, lake, or another river. When a river reaches an ocean, the water slows and sand, clay, and sediment in the water sink. When the sediment builds up, it makes a landform called a **delta**. In Florida, the Apalachicola River supplies sand to St. Vincent's Island, a barrier island and wildlife refuge.

☑ READING CHECK **Compare and Contrast** How are dunes and deltas similar and different?

....

....

17

Modeling Landforms

Before modern technology, scientists and mapmakers studied the land and drew maps by hand. They spent hundreds of hours walking over landforms or sailing along coastlines to **model** what they saw. Then people used a process called surveying. In **surveying**, mapmakers determine distances and elevations using instruments and the principles of geometry. Today, people use computers to create topographic and other maps from aerial photography and satellite imagery.

Topographic Maps

Imagine that you are in a plane flying high above the United States. How does it look? A topographic map portrays the surface features of an area as if being viewed from above. Topographic maps provide accurate information on the elevation, relief, and slope of the ground, as shown in **Figure 5**.

Contour Lines

Topographic maps have contour lines to show elevation, relief, and slope. A contour line connects points of equal elevation. Contour lines also show how steep or gradual a slope is. Contour lines that are far apart represent flat areas or areas with gradual slopes. Lines that are close together represent areas with steep slopes.

The change in elevation from one contour line to the next is called a contour interval. On a given map, the contour interval is always consistent. Every fifth contour line is known as an index contour. These lines are darker and heavier than the other lines.

Topographic Map of Mt. Grinnell

Figure 5 The contour lines on the map can be used to determine a feature's elevation. Use the contour lines to determine the elevation of Mt. Grinnell.

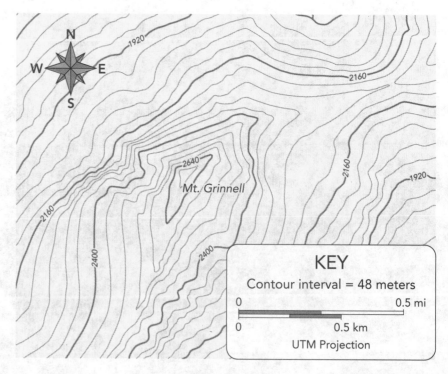

KEY

Contour interval = 48 meters

0   0.5 mi

0   0.5 km

UTM Projection

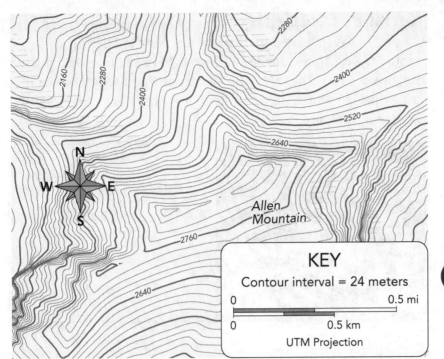

Shape of Contour Lines

Figure 6 The area around Allen Mountain has many features. Circle the hilltops. Mark the steepest slopes with an *X*.

KEY

Contour interval = 24 meters

0   0.5 mi

0   0.5 km

UTM Projection

👆 **INTERACTIVITY**

Investigate how constructive and destructive forces affect Earth's landforms.

Reading a Topographic Map In the United States, the scale of many topographic maps is 1 centimeter on the map for every 0.24 kilometers on the ground. This scale allows mapmakers to show land features such as rivers and coastlines. Large human-made structures, such as airports and highways, appear as outlines, while small structures, such as houses, are represented with symbols.

To find the elevation of a feature on the map in **Figure 6**, begin at an index contour line and count the number of lines up or down the feature. The shape of contour lines also provides information. V-shaped contour lines pointing away from a summit indicate a ridge line. V-shaped contour lines pointing toward a summit indicate a valley. A contour line that forms a closed loop indicates a hilltop. A closed loop with dashes inside indicates a depression, or hollow in the ground.

Model It !

A map is a way to model Earth. What features are modeled by the topographic map in **Figure 6**?

SEP Use Mathematics ✏ Use the topographic map to create a drawing of the features it represents. Use the contour lines to help determine whether the area has a steep or gradual elevation. Be sure to label your illustration with the elevation of each feature.

Aerial Photography
When photographs are taken with cameras mounted in airplanes, it is called aerial photography. As the airplane flies, the camera takes pictures of strips of land. These picture strips are fitted together like a large puzzle to form an accurate picture of a large area of land, as shown in **Figure 7**.

Aerial Photograph
Figure 7 🖊 Mapmakers use aerial photographs such as this one to create a map. Use the photo to make a street map of the neighborhood in the photograph. Be sure to add your own street names.

Satellite Imagery
With the creation of computers, mapping has become easier and more accurate. Mapmakers can make maps of Earth using computers that interpret satellite data. Mapping satellites use electronic devices to collect data about the land surface. Pictures of the surface based on these data are called satellite images. These images are made up of pixels, and each pixel has information about the color and brightness of a part of Earth's surface, as shown in **Figure 8**.

Satellites orbit Earth collecting and storing data. Then, computers use the data to create images. Satellite images show details including plants, soil, rock, water, snow, and ice that cover Earth's surface.

Satellite Image of North America
Figure 8 🖊 Scientists and mapmakers identify special features on an image by their color and shape. For example, forests appear green, water may be blue or black, and snow is white. Draw an *X* to show where your state is.

Interpret Photos Write about the features you see in the satellite image.

....

....

....

....

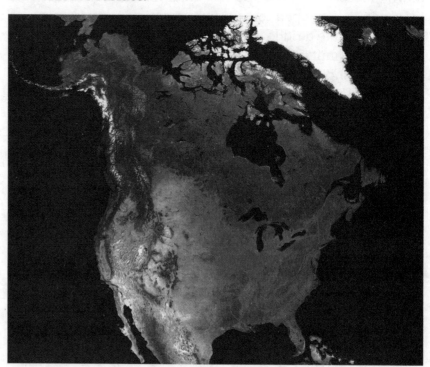

GPS The Global Positioning System, or GPS, is a navigational system that uses satellite signals to fix the location of a radio receiver on Earth. GPS helps anyone with a receiver locate his or her position anywhere on or above Earth.

You may have used GPS on a phone or in a car to navigate, but do you know how it works? Twenty-four orbiting satellites continuously send their current location and time to a GPS receiver on Earth. A user's receiver, such as a phone, needs information from at least three satellites to determine its location.

GIS A Geographic Information System, or GIS, is a system of computer hardware and software used to produce interactive maps. GIS uses GPS, satellite images, statistics about an area, and other maps to display and analyze geographic data.

The different types of information stored in a GIS are called data layers. The data layers help scientists and city planners to solve problems by understanding patterns, relationships, and trends. **Figure 9** shows how GIS could be used to determine a neighborhood's flood risk by analyzing data layers about the location of a river, its floodplain boundary, and the streets in a neighborhood.

INTERACTIVITY

Explore how maps can help solve problems.

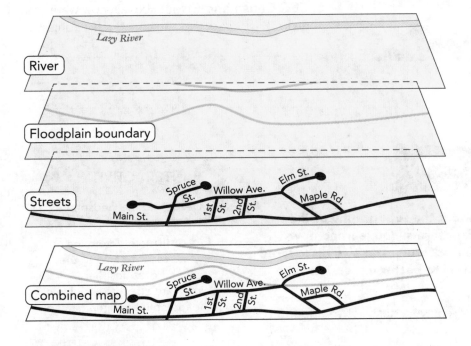

GIS Map
Figure 9 🖉 A GIS map has many data layers that can be used to analyze how different systems interact. Shade in the floodplain on the combined map. Where should a city planner avoid building houses? Why?

....

....

✅ READING CHECK **Write Explanatory Texts** Explain ways in which GPS and GIS are more useful than a topographic map.

....

....

....

1. Define What is topography?

....

....

....

....

2. Identify A mountain is a landform with both

high .... and high ....

3. SEP Use Models ✏ Match each set of contour lines to the correct drawing.

4. Compare and Contrast Compare and contrast constructive and destructive forces.

....

....

....

....

....

....

5. Infer The owner of a car wash wants to open a new location in a different neighborhood. How could the owner use GIS to figure out where to put the new car wash? Explain what information should be included in the data layers.

....

....

....

....

6. CCC Cause and Effect Explain how water can be both a destructive and constructive force.

....

....

....

Quest CHECK-IN

In this lesson, you learned about the topography of the geosphere and the various landforms. You learned how different forces shape these landforms. You also discovered how scientists model landforms to better understand the topography.

CCC Systems How might a fire have a destructive effect on the geosphere?

....

....

....

....

INTERACTIVITY

Disrupting the Geosphere

Go online to determine how the interactions among the geosphere, atmosphere, and biosphere affect the course of the forest fire and the damage it causes.

A DARING BRIDGE

Do you know how to build a bridge with some tough budget and environmental constraints? You engineer it! Plans for the Bixby Bridge in California show us how.

The Challenge: To design a cost-effective bridge across a canyon that withstands the elements.

Phenomenon Every winter, people in Big Sur, California, were trapped. Bad weather made the Old Coast Road impossible to travel. That changed in the 1930s when the state built a bridge across the canyon cut by Bixby Creek.

In designing the bridge, engineers weighed its impact on the environment. Then they considered costs and appearance. The country had entered the Great Depression. Funds were scarce, and a steel bridge would be costly. Also, a steel bridge so close to the Pacific Ocean would rust.

Finally, the engineers decided on an uncovered arch bridge 713 feet long and more than 260 feet above the canyon floor. They used concrete—45,000 sacks of it. Its appearance fit better alongside the area's stone cliffs. This design was also much less expensive. The Bixby Bridge reached completion on time and under budget—a success for any building project!

VIDEO

Learn how engineers considered each sphere when building the Bixby Bridge.

During the 1930s and 1940s, the lack of good roads and bridges could sometimes make traveling by car impossible.

DESIGN CHALLENGE

Can you design a bridge? Go to the Engineering Design Notebook to find out!

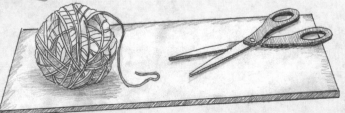

③ The Hydrosphere

Guiding Questions

- Where and in what features is water found on Earth?
- How does water cycle through Earth's systems?

Connection

Literacy Determine Central Ideas

MS-ESS2-4

HANDS-ON LAB

uInvestigate Model the distribution of water on Earth.

Vocabulary

water cycle
evaporation
transpiration
condensation
precipitation
watershed
aquifer
well

Academic Vocabulary

process

Connect It !

🖉 **Circle the different areas of water in this photo.**

Infer Why do human practices depend upon and benefit from water?

....

....

....

SEP Apply Scientific Reasoning Why is water important to our planet?

....

....

....

The Water Cycle

Without water, life as we know it would not exist. As shown in **Figure 1**, water is an important characteristic of Earth. All living things require water to live. Fortunately, Earth has its own built-in water recycling system: the water cycle.

The **water cycle** is the continuous process by which water moves from Earth's surface to the atmosphere and back again. This movement is driven by energy from the sun and by gravity. In the water cycle, water moves through the geosphere, the biosphere, the hydrosphere, and the atmosphere.

Evaporation The sun heats up the surface of bodies of water and causes water molecules to undergo a change. The process by which molecules at the surface of a liquid absorb enough energy to change to a gas is called **evaporation**. Water constantly evaporates from the surfaces of bodies of water.

Elements of the geosphere and biosphere can also add water vapor to the atmosphere. Water evaporates from soil in the geosphere. Animals in the biosphere release water vapor as they breathe. Water even evaporates from your skin.

Plants also play a role in this step of the water cycle. Plants draw in water from the soil through their roots. Eventually the water vapor is given off through the leaves in a process called **transpiration**.

Importance of Water
Figure 1 Water makes life on Earth possible.

The Water Cycle

Figure 2 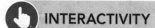 This diagram shows some of the major processes that make up the water cycle. Draw arrows to show the way that water moves through the cycle. Then, in the blank spaces, write the process that is at work.

INTERACTIVITY

Review all of the processes of the water cycle.

Literacy Connection

Determine Central Ideas
As you read, underline the central idea of each paragraph. Note how this idea is developed through examples and details.

Condensation After a water molecule evaporates into the atmosphere, warm air carries the water molecule upward. **Condensation** is the process by which water vapor becomes liquid water. As water vapor rises into the colder air, some water vapor cools and condenses into liquid or solid water. Droplets of liquid water and ice crystals collect around solid particles in the air, forming clouds. Eventually, this results in precipitation.

Precipitation As more water vapor condenses, the water droplets and ice crystals grow larger. Eventually, they become so heavy that gravity causes them to fall back to Earth in the form of precipitation. Water that forms in clouds and falls to Earth as rain, snow, hail, or sleet is called **precipitation**. Once it falls, it collects in rivers, lakes, and streams. It is also absorbed by the soil in the geosphere. Precipitation is the source of almost all fresh water on and below Earth's surface.

For millions of years, the total amount of water cycling through the Earth's system has remained fairly constant—the rates of evaporation and precipitation are balanced. That means that the water you use today is the same water that your ancestors used.

☑ **READING CHECK** **Draw Evidence** The biosphere interacts with the hydrosphere within the water cycle. Cite one example of that interaction.

....

....

....

Distribution of Earth's Water

Most of the water in the hydrosphere—roughly 97 percent—is salt water found mostly in the ocean. Only 3 percent is fresh water, as shown in **Figure 3**.

Fresh Water Of the 3 percent that is fresh water, about two-thirds is frozen in huge masses of ice near the North and South poles. Much of Earth's fresh water is frozen into thickened ice masses called glaciers. Massive glacial ice sheets cover most of Greenland and Antarctica.

About a third of Earth's fresh water is underground. A tiny fraction of fresh water occurs in lakes and rivers. An even tinier fraction is found in the atmosphere, most of it in the form of invisible water vapor, the gaseous form of water.

Most precipitation falls directly into the ocean. Of the precipitation that falls on land, most evaporates. A small amount of the remaining water runs off the surface into streams and lakes in a **process** called runoff, but most of it seeps into the ground. After a long time, this groundwater eventually comes to the surface and evaporates again.

Salt Water Atlantic, Indian, Pacific, and Arctic are the names for the different parts of the ocean. The Pacific Ocean is the largest, covering an area greater than all the land on Earth. Smaller saltwater bodies are called seas. Seas are generally inland and landlocked. A small percentage of Earth's salt water is found in some saline lakes.

HANDS-ON LAB

u**Investigate** Model the distribution of water on Earth.

Academic Vocabulary

A process is a series of actions or operations leading toward a particular result. List some processes you are familiar with in your daily life.

....

....

....

....

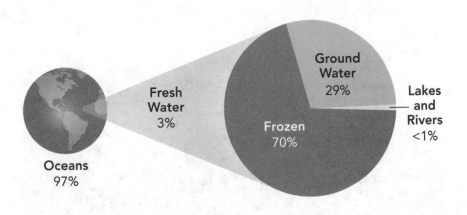

Water Resources
Figure 3 Most of the water on Earth is salt water in the ocean.

Ground Water 29%

Fresh Water 3%

Lakes and Rivers <1%

Frozen 70%

Oceans 97%

Reflect NASA satellite data show that the ice sheets are melting at a rate of about 350 billion tons of ice each year, which is far above historic averages. What do you think is causing this to happen? What effect would this increased amount of ice melt have on the ocean?

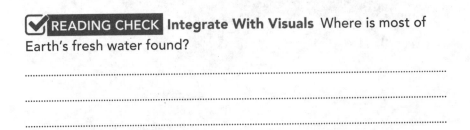

✓ **READING CHECK** **Integrate With Visuals** Where is most of Earth's fresh water found?

....

....

....

The Mississippi River
Figure 4 Many tributaries contribute to the Mississippi River.

 VIDEO

Discover how an aquaculture manager helps meet the needs of people while protecting the habitats of living things.

Watersheds

Figure 5 ✏ This map shows the watersheds of some large rivers in the United States. Draw a line on the map to represent the Great Divide. Use arrows to show the direction in which the water flows on each side of the divide.

Surface Water

Surface water includes all the water found on the surface of Earth. The ocean, rivers, lakes, and ponds are all part of the surface water in the hydrosphere.

Rivers Even large rivers, such as the Mississippi River or St. Johns River, start as a trickle of water that originates from a source—an underground stream, runoff from rain, or melting snow or ice. Gravity causes these tiny streams to flow downhill. These small streams join others to form a larger stream. Larger streams join others to form a river that flows into the ocean. The streams and smaller rivers that feed into a main river are called tributaries. A river and all the tributaries that flow into it make up a river system, as shown in **Figure 4**.

Watersheds The land area that supplies water to a river system is called a **watershed**. When rivers join another river system, the areas they drain become part of the largest river's watershed. **Figure 5** shows the major watersheds that cover the United States.

Divides Watersheds stay separated from each other by a ridge of land called a divide. Streams on each side of the divide flow in different directions. The Great Divide, the longest divide in North America, follows the Rocky Mountains. West of this divide, water flows toward the Pacific Ocean. Some water stays in the Great Basin between the Rocky and Sierra Nevada Mountains. East of the divide, water flows toward the Mississippi River and into the Gulf of Mexico, joining rivers flowing from the Appalachian Mountains.

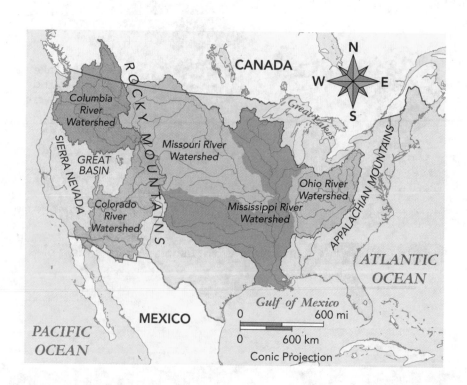

Ponds and Lakes

Ponds and lakes form when water collects in hollows and low-lying areas of land. Unlike streams and rivers, ponds and lakes contain mostly still water. Ponds are smaller and shallower than lakes. Like other bodies of water, lakes and ponds are supplied by rainfall, melting snow and ice, and runoff. Some are fed by rivers or groundwater.

Lakes, such as the ones in **Figure 6**, form through several natural processes. When a river bends, a new channel may form, cutting off a loop to form an oxbow lake. Some lakes, such as the Great Lakes, formed in depressions created by ice sheets that melted at the end of the Ice Age. Other lakes were created by movements of Earth's crust that formed long, deep valleys called rift valleys. Lakes can also form in the empty craters of volcanoes.

☑ READING CHECK **Summarize** How do river systems, watersheds, and divides interact?

....

....

....

....

....

....

👆 INTERACTIVITY

Discover the best site on which to locate a fish farm.

Lakes in Mountains
Figure 6 Lakes are important because they hold some of Earth's fresh water.

Plan It ❗

Building a Reservoir

SEP Design Solutions 🖊 In order to increase the benefit from the water cycle, humans alter it by building reservoirs, which store water. Do some research to help you plan how to build a reservoir in your region of the country. Use the space provided to draw a diagram showing the features of your reservoir. Write out the steps of your plan below.

....

....

....

....

Groundwater

Figure 7 ✏ This diagram shows how water travels underground. Add arrows to identify the paths that water takes.

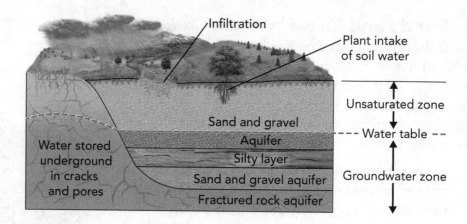

Infiltration
Plant intake of soil water
Unsaturated zone
--- Water table ---
Sand and gravel
Aquifer
Silty layer
Sand and gravel aquifer
Fractured rock aquifer
Groundwater zone
Water stored underground in cracks and pores

👆 **INTERACTIVITY**

Explore how the Floridan aquifer formed and describe its importance today.

▶ **VIDEO**

Learn more about the role of groundwater in the water cycle.

Groundwater

A large portion of fresh water in the hydrosphere is underground, as shown in **Figure 7**. Water that fills the cracks and spaces in soil and rock layers is called groundwater. Far more fresh water is located underground than in all of Earth's rivers and lakes.

Aquifers As precipitation falls to Earth, it moves through the soil and the small spaces within underground rock layers. These layers contain air as well as water, so they are not saturated, or filled, with water. This top layer is called the unsaturated zone.

Eventually, the water reaches a level where the openings in the layers are filled with water, or saturated. The upper level of the saturated zone is called the water table. Below the saturated zone there are layers of rock that hold water called **aquifers**.

Aquifers range in size from a small patch to an area the size of several states. Aquifers and other groundwater sources provide 55 percent of the drinking water for the United States. In rural areas, aquifers provide as much as 99 percent of the water used.

Wells People can get groundwater from an aquifer by digging a well that reaches below the water table. A **well** is a hole sunk into the earth to reach a supply of water. Long ago, people dug wells by hand and used buckets to bring up the water. Today, most wells are created with drilling equipment and the water is retrieved using mechanical pumps that run on electricity.

✓ READING CHECK **Determine Central Ideas** What is an aquifer?

....

....

....

....

Exploring the Ocean

There are several ways that the ocean is unique in the hydrosphere. The water in Earth's ocean varies in salinity, temperature, and depth.

Salinity The total amount of dissolved salts in a sample of water is the salinity. Near the ocean's surface, rain, snow, and melting ice add fresh water, lowering the salinity. Evaporation, on the other hand, increases salinity. Salinity is also higher near the poles because the forming of sea ice leaves some salt behind in the seawater.

Salinity affects ocean water in different ways. For instance, fresh water freezes at 0°C but ocean water freezes at about –1.9°C because the salt interferes with the formation of ice. Salt water also has a higher density than fresh water. Therefore, seawater lifts, or buoys up, less dense objects floating in it.

Temperature The broad surface of the ocean absorbs energy from the sun. Temperatures at the surface of the ocean vary with location and the seasons. Near the equator, surface ocean temperatures often reach 25°C, about room temperature. The temperatures drop as you travel away from the equator.

Depth The ocean is very deep—3.8 kilometers deep on average. That's more than twice as deep as the Grand Canyon. As you descend through the ocean, the water temperature decreases. Water pressure, the force exerted by the weight of water, increases by 1 bar, the air pressure at sea level, with each 10 meters of depth. Use **Figure 8** to explore temperature, pressure, and depth.

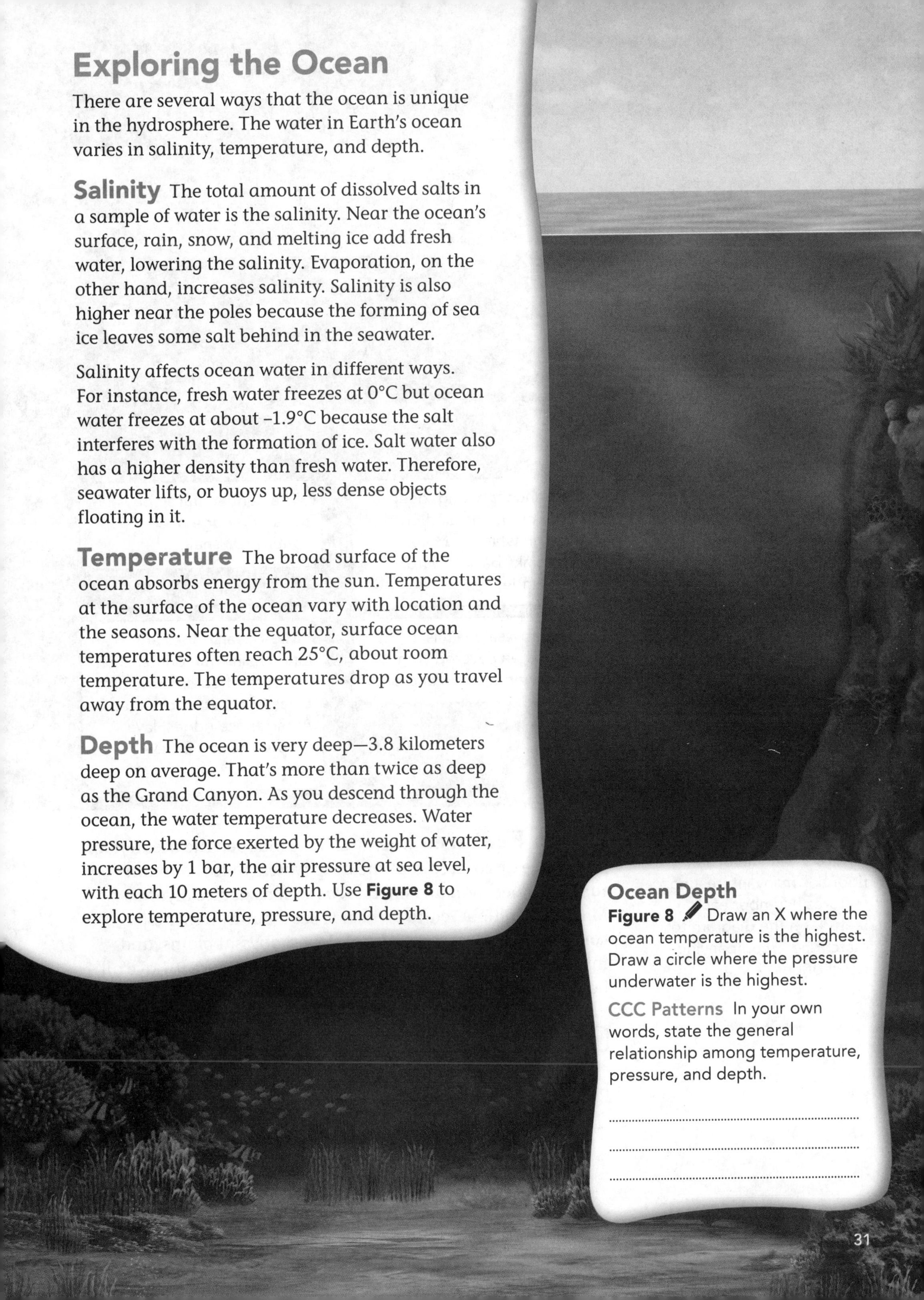

Ocean Depth

Figure 8 🖊 Draw an X where the ocean temperature is the highest. Draw a circle where the pressure underwater is the highest.

CCC Patterns In your own words, state the general relationship among temperature, pressure, and depth.

....

....

....

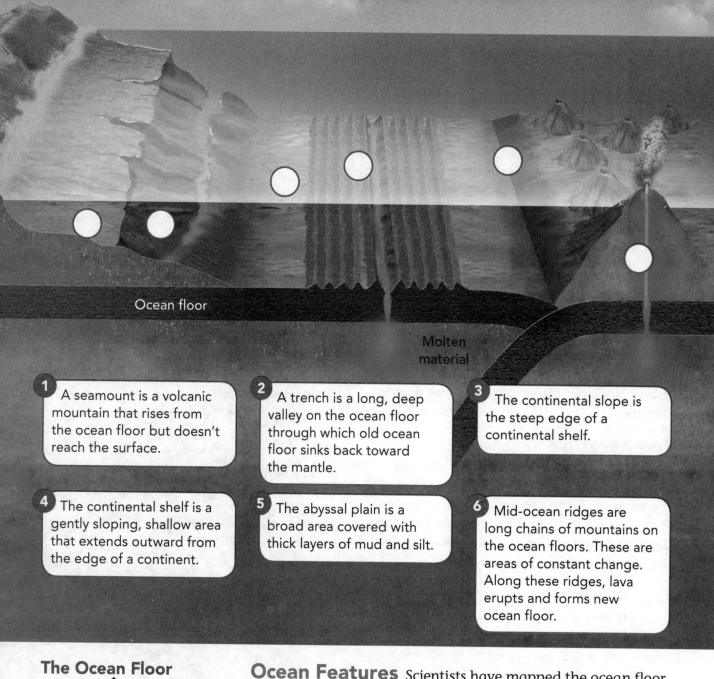

Ocean floor

Molten material

1. A seamount is a volcanic mountain that rises from the ocean floor but doesn't reach the surface.

2. A trench is a long, deep valley on the ocean floor through which old ocean floor sinks back toward the mantle.

3. The continental slope is the steep edge of a continental shelf.

4. The continental shelf is a gently sloping, shallow area that extends outward from the edge of a continent.

5. The abyssal plain is a broad area covered with thick layers of mud and silt.

6. Mid-ocean ridges are long chains of mountains on the ocean floors. These are areas of constant change. Along these ridges, lava erupts and forms new ocean floor.

The Ocean Floor

Figure 9 ✏ The ocean floor has many interesting features. Number each feature on the diagram to match the accompanying descriptions.

Ocean Features Scientists have mapped the ocean floor. They have discovered that the deep waters hide mountain ranges bigger than any on land, as well as deep canyons. Major ocean floor features include seamounts, trenches, continental shelves, continental slopes, abyssal plains, and mid-ocean ridges. These features, shown in **Figure 9**, have all been formed by the interaction of Earth's plates.

✅ **READING CHECK** **Draw Conclusions** How do the temperature and pressure most likely differ at the top of a seamount and the bottom of a trench?

....

....

....

....

MS-ESS2-4

1. CCC Systems What are the important processes in the water cycle?

....
....
....

2. CCC Structure and Function What are the components of a river system?

....
....
....
....

3. Summarize What are the main features of the ocean floor?

....
....
....
....
....
....

4. SEP Communicate Information How does the interaction between the hydrosphere and the geosphere affect the supply of drinking water?

....
....
....
....
....
....

5. Compare and Contrast ✏ Create a Venn diagram comparing fresh water and salt water.

Quest CHECK-IN

In this lesson, you learned how the water of the hydrosphere is cycled and how it interacts with the other spheres. You also learned about the characteristics of each portion of the hydrosphere, including surface water, ocean water, and groundwater.

CCC Cause and Effect How might a natural disaster, such as a forest fire, affect the elements of the hydrosphere?

....
....
....
....

👆 INTERACTIVITY

Impact on the Hydrosphere

Go online to examine how the hydrosphere interacts with other spheres and the effect of a forest fire on those interactions. Then review the data and finalize your predictions about the fire's damage.

1989

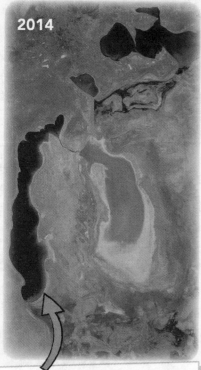

2014

The remaining areas of water now cover only 10 to 25 percent of the former surface area. The volume of water has been reduced by 90 percent.

The CASE of the
Shrinking Sea

The Aral Sea in Central Asia was once the fourth largest lake in the world, and it supported many fisheries and shipping lines. Bordered by the countries of Uzbekistan and Kazakhstan, the lake is fed by water from melting glaciers and the rivers of the Aral Sea Basin, which flow from five countries in the region.

But the Aral Sea has been rapidly disappearing since the 1960s. As the population in the area grew to more than 60 million, people diverted major rivers flowing into the lake for agricultural and industrial use. However, up to one quarter of this diverted water was wasted due to poor management and planning. This wasted water was either absorbed by dry desert soil surrounding the lake or flowed into unused run-off ditches. Additionally, the rate of evaporation from the Aral Sea has increased, contributing to its disappearance.

In the past 50 years, the water levels have dropped so rapidly that the lake has fragmented into several smaller bodies of water separated by barren desert in between.

Effects of a Disappearing Sea

As the lake evaporates and shrinks, its salinity increases. Between the 1960s and the 1980s, the salt concentration of the Aral Sea increased dramatically, killing wildlife and destroying the fishing trade. The concentration of salt is so high in some areas that efforts to reintroduce fish have failed. Concentrated salt, minerals, and pollutants from the now-exposed sea floor are whipped into sandstorms that also threaten the health of the human population in the area.

To improve the conditions in the area, some water management efforts started in the 1990s. Then, in 2005, the Kok-Aral Dam was built to keep water from the northern fragment from flowing to the southern fragment. The dam was a success and the North Aral Sea rose more than 3 meters in the first year. Surveyors hope that in the future the water levels in the north will rise to the point that they can begin to let water flow to the South Aral Sea as well.

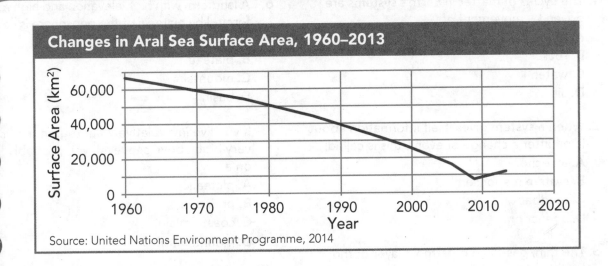

Source: United Nations Environment Programme, 2014

Use the graph to answer the following questions.

1. **CCC Patterns** Describe any patterns you see in the graph.

   ....

   ....

2. **Predict** What do you think the data for the Aral Sea surface area might look like in 2020? Why?

   ....

   ....

3. **SEP Construct Explanations** How have human actions and the impact of the water cycle affected the Aral Sea?

   ....

   ....

   ....

4. **SEP Design Solutions** What are some strategies you can think of to conserve water and stabilize the decline of the Aral Sea?

   ....

   ....

☑TOPIC 1 Review and Assess

① Matter and Energy in Earth's System

MS-ESS2-1

1. The cycles of matter in Earth's systems are driven by movement of
   A. heat.
   B. rock.
   C. water.
   D. air.

2. When a system gives itself information about itself after a change or event, this is called
   A. an echo.
   B. system response.
   C. feedback.
   D. a reaction.

3. The thin, gas-filled outermost layer of the Earth system is called the
   A. cryosphere.
   B. atmosphere.
   C. geosphere.
   D. hydrosphere.

4. In the ...., water exists in its solid form as ice.

5. CCC Systems Give an example of an interaction involving the cycling of matter between two or more spheres.

   ....
   ....
   ....
   ....
   ....
   ....
   ....
   ....
   ....

② Surface Features in the Geosphere

MS-ESS2-1

6. A landform with high elevation and high relief formed by material of the geosphere is called a
   A. plain.
   B. plateau.
   C. mountain.
   D. basin.

7. If you live in a relatively flat region that is not very high above sea level, you probably live on a
   A. plateau.
   B. prairie.
   C. coastal plain.
   D. mountaintop.

8. Which type of map image would you use if you wanted to represent plant density across the United States?
   A. satellite imagery
   B. aerial photography
   C. topographic map
   D. relief map

9. With ...., you can find your precise location on a digital map if your device can receive signals from three satellites. A .... map is a low-tech tool for visualizing the contours and elevations of a landform.

10. SEP Engage in Argument Write a brief proposal for why GPS technology and surveying should be used to study changes on a low-lying part of the coast.

    ....
    ....
    ....
    ....

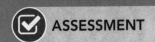
3 The Hydrosphere

MS-ESS2-4

11. Which is not a part of the hydrosphere?
A. sediment
B. pond
C. rain
D. ice

12. When ocean water reaches the poles, some of it turns to ice. Some salt is trapped between ice crystals, but most is left behind in the unfrozen seawater. This causes an increase in
A. evaporation. B. salinity.
C. pressure. D. temperature.

13. About 97 percent of the hydrosphere is
A. salt water in lakes, seas, and the ocean.
B. water vapor in the atmosphere.
C. fresh water in ice and snow.
D. also part of the cryosphere.

14. .... from plants and .... from bodies of water both add water vapor to the ....

15. In this photo, the .... is interacting with the .... by wearing down the rocks as the water flows.

16. CCC Cause and Effect Describe how groundwater is replenished.

....
....
....
....
....

17. CCC System Models Suppose you have a teakettle boiling on a hotplate next to a window. It is a cold morning, and as steam from the kettle hits the window, it forms ice. What parts of the water cycle are you modeling?

....
....
....

18. SEP Develop Models 🖊 How might water from a lake move through the water cycle and eventually fall as rain? Draw a diagram to model the cycle.

MS-ESS2-4

Evidence-Based Assessment

Scientists have been monitoring the enormous volumes of ice at Earth's poles with curiosity and concern. In western Antarctica, the ice shelves are deteriorating. An ice shelf acts as a dam between land-based glaciers and the ocean. As a shelf crumbles into the ocean, glacial ice behind the ice shelf can flow more freely from higher elevations. The collapsing ice shelf, which floats on the ocean, does not directly contribute to sea level rise. However, scientists predict that the increased flow of glacial ice and meltwater from land will contribute to a global sea level rise of two meters by 2100.

The graph provides data about the volume of ice lost at four different glacier systems.

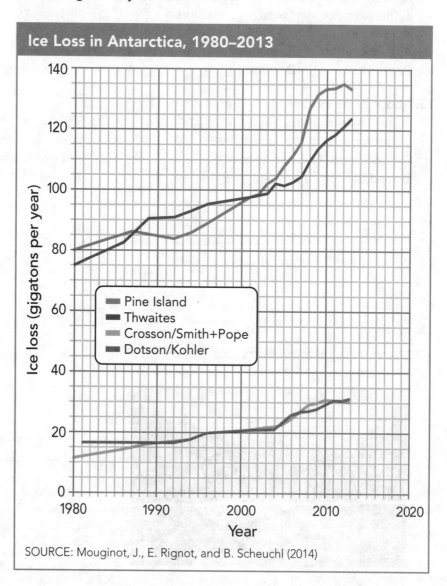

Ice Loss in Antarctica, 1980–2013

Legend:
- Pine Island
- Thwaites
- Crosson/Smith+Pope
- Dotson/Kohler

Y-axis: Ice loss (gigatons per year)
X-axis: Year

SOURCE: Mouginot, J., E. Rignot, and B. Scheuchl (2014)

1. **CCC Stability and Change** What is the overall trend in ice loss at the four locations?
   A. Ice loss has been increasing at all four locations, but the rate has been getting higher since about 2000.
   B. Ice loss has remained at a steady rate at all four locations.
   C. Ice loss was decreasing at all four locations until 2005, when it began to increase.
   D. Ice loss has been decreasing at a steady rate at all four locations.

2. **SEP Use Mathematics** Which location lost the most ice in 2013? Approximately how much ice was lost from the four locations in 2013? Show your work.

   ....
   ....
   ....
   ....
   ....
   ....
   ....
   ....
   ....

3. **CCC Cause and Effect** What role does the sun play in driving the water cycle in Antarctica?

   ....
   ....
   ....
   ....
   ....
   ....
   ....
   ....

4. **SEP Engage in Argument** Average temperatures on the Antarctic Peninsula have risen 3°C over the last 50 years. If this trend continues, what effect would it have on the water cycle in Antarctica? In your answer, explain the impact on ice flows.

   ....
   ....
   ....
   ....
   ....
   ....
   ....

Quest FINDINGS

Complete the Quest!

Phenomenon Determine the best medium for presenting your findings, such as a map or a multimedia presentation.

CCC Systems How does a forest fire demonstrate how the different spheres of Earth interact with each other?

....
....
....
....
....
....
....

👆 **INTERACTIVITY**

Reflect on Forest Fires

MS-ESS2-4

Modeling a Watershed

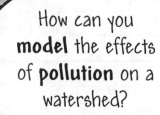

How can you **model** the effects of **pollution** on a watershed?

Background

Phenomenon A factory has released pollutants into a nearby river. You discovered dead fish far downstream from the factory. But the factory claims that it can't be responsible because the fish were found so far away. You have been asked to help biologists demonstrate that when contaminated water enters one part of a watershed, it can affect the entire watershed.

In this investigation, you will model the effects of pollution on surface water in a watershed and demonstrate the importance of protecting watershed areas.

Materials

(per group)

- small wooden or plastic blocks
- paper or plastic drinking cups
- newspaper
- markers
- craft sticks
- plastic CD cases
- light paper
- aluminum foil
- plastic wrap
- large pan
- water
- red food coloring
- metric ruler
- tape
- digital camera (optional)
- goggles
- apron
- gloves

Procedure

HANDS-ON LAB

⊔**Demonstrate** Go online for a downloadable worksheet of this lab.

☐ 1. Use the materials provided by your teacher to design and build a model watershed for your demonstration. Use a camera or drawings to record and analyze information to show how pollution affects an entire watershed.

☐ 2. Consider the following questions before you begin planning your model:

  - How can the materials help you to model a watershed?

  - How will you form highlands in your model?

  - How can you include streams and rivers in your model?

  - How can you use food coloring to represent the effects of pollution on surface water in the watershed?

  - What are some ways that a watershed can be polluted?

☐ 3. Once you have worked out a design, draw a sketch of your model. Label the objects in your model and identify the materials you are using.

☐ 4. Write a short procedure that details the steps you will follow to model how pollution can affect surface water in a watershed.

☐ 5. Once your teacher has approved your design and procedure, carry out the investigation. If possible, use a camera to photograph your model during the investigation. Record observations about how your model represents the effects of pollution in a watershed.

Sketch Design and sketch your model here.

Observations

Analyze and Interpret Data

1. Claim What other human activity takes place in the watersheds that might lead to pollution?

....

....

....

2. Evidence Describe the path that the food coloring took through your model. What does the pattern of the food coloring's path tell you about the effect of pollution on surface water in a watershed? Based on your observations and evidence, could the factory's pollution have caused the fish to die?

....

....

....

....

3. Reasoning Explain the importance of laws that restrict and punish individuals or businesses that pollute healthy watersheds. Include a description of any cause-and-effect relationships that you think scientists might observe when pollutants are introduced into a watershed area. Use your model and your observations in this lab as evidence for your answer.

....

....

....

....

....

4. SEP Identify Limitations Compare your model to other models. How can you improve your model based on other examples? What parts of a watershed, if any, are missing from your model?

....

....

....

Minerals and Rocks in the Geosphere

NGSS PERFORMANCE EXPECTATION

MS-ESS2-1 Develop a model to describe the cycling of Earth's materials and the flow of energy that drives this process.

GO ONLINE
to access your
digital course

 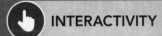 VIDEO

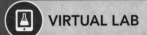 INTERACTIVITY

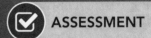 VIRTUAL LAB

 ASSESSMENT

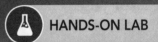 eTEXT

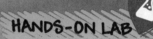 HANDS-ON LAB

What caused
this rock to look
like this?

HANDS-ON LAB

иConnect Explore and model Earth's
structure.

The Essential Question

What events form Earth's rocks?

SEP Construct Explanations Shiprock is a rock formation in New Mexico that stands about 480 meters (about 1,600 feet) tall. How do you think this rock formed?

....

....

....

....

....

Quest KICKOFF

How can you depict Earth processes in a movie script?

Phenomenon A movie producer is working on an exciting new adventure film. Much of the action takes place not in space, not on Earth, but *under* the surface of Earth. The producer wants to present a realistic view of this world, so she hires a science consultant to help get the facts right. In this problem-based Quest activity, you will help evaluate and revise movie scripts whose plots involve action that takes place within Earth. Based on your research and understanding of Earth's structure, you will suggest changes that reflect accurate science. In the Findings activity, you will reflect on how accurately movies depict scientific facts.

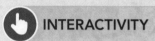

INTERACTIVITY

Science in the Movies

MS-ESS2-1 Develop a model to describe the cycling of Earth's materials and the flow of energy that drives this process.

NBC LEARN ▶ VIDEO

After watching the Quest Kickoff video and reacting to some movie scenes, think about a scientific falsehood that you have seen in a movie. How do you suggest changing the script to reflect the science accurately?

The scene and its false science

....
....
....
....

How the scene should be changed

....
....
....
....

Quest CHECK-IN

IN LESSON 1

What is the structure of Earth's mantle and core? How could a movie accurately depict these regions inside Earth?

INTERACTIVITY

The Deep Drill

Quest CHECK-INS

IN LESSON 2

How do stalactites and stalagmites form? Model the formation of these structures.

HANDS-ON LAB

Make Your Own Stalactites and Stalagmites

Quest CHECK-IN

IN LESSON 3

What are the three types of rocks and how do they form? Consider how different types of rock form and represent that information accurately in a movie script.

INTERACTIVITY

Rocky Business

The 1959 movie *Journey to the Center of the Earth* was based on Jules Verne's novel, published in 1864. In the story, a professor and several other characters travel through the center of Earth, entering through a volcano in Iceland and exiting through a volcano in Italy.

Quest CHECK-IN

IN LESSON 4

What processes affect rock formation? Understand different rock cycle processes and appropriately depict those processes in a script.

👆 **INTERACTIVITY**

The Rock Cyclers

Quest FINDINGS

Complete the Quest!

Now that you have revised movie scripts to be more scientifically accurate, consider how you will view the science in other movies differently.

👆 **INTERACTIVITY**

Reflect on Science in Movies

uConnect Lab

MS-ESS2-1

Build a Model of Earth

How can you **develop a scale model** of Earth?

Background

Phenomenon As a summer camp counselor, you challenge the campers to show energy cycling inside Earth by making a scale model of Earth. Recalling that Earth has four main layers—inner core, outer core, mantle, and crust—you will instruct the campers to develop and construct a sample scale model of Earth that shows the flow of energy.

Develop a Model

1. **CCC Energy and Matter** Use the following information to help you develop your model. The temperature inside Earth increases with depth. Earth's mantle is heated by high temperatures near the core, causing it to sink and rise with the constant cycle of convection currents. These convection currents carry hot, solid rock up toward the surface where it cools and sinks.

2. **CCC Scale, Proportion, Quantity** Use the information in the table to determine what scale you will use for your model. Record your scale.

Component	Actual Thickness	Scaled Thickness
Earth's Radius	6,370 km	
Inner Core	1,220 km	
Outer Core	2,260 km	
Mantle	2,880 km	
Crust	30 km	

Materials

(per group)
- plastic knife
- different colors of modeling clay
- toothpicks
- colored pencils
- wax paper
- ruler

Safety

Be sure to follow all safety procedures provided by your teacher. The Safety Appendix of your textbook provides more details about the safety icons.

3. **SEP Develop a Model** Use the provided materials. Decide how to make your model using the information from step 1 and the scale you calculated. Record your plan for your model. Draw a sketch to help you build your model. Include labels for the layers, the thicknesses, and convection currents. Show your plan to your teacher for approval.

4. Build your model on a piece of wax paper.

Plan and Sketch

Analyze and Conclude

1. **SEP Use Models** Using your model as supporting evidence, describe the structure of Earth, including the relative thickness of each layer.

....

....

....

2. **CCC Cause and Effect** Suppose the crust in your model were not solid, but was broken into several large sections. What effect might this movement of material in the mantle have on the crust?

....

....

....

HANDS-ON LAB

Connect Go online for a downloadable worksheet of this lab.

47B

① Earth's Interior

Guiding Questions

- How do geologists study Earth's layered interior?
- What roles do heat and pressure in Earth's interior play in the cycling of matter?
- What are the patterns and effects of convection in Earth's mantle?

Connections

Literacy Translate Information

Math Construct Graphs

MS-ESS2-1

HANDS-ON LAB

ⁿInvestigate Explore how convection works.

Vocabulary

seismic wave
crust
mantle
outer core
inner core

Academic Vocabulary

evidence
elements

Connect It !

What do you observe about the rock shown in Figure 1?

Determine Differences How do the xenoliths compare to the surrounding rock?

....

Apply Scientific Reasoning How might xenoliths help geologists understand Earth's interior?

....

....

Learning About Earth's Interior

How do we study Earth's interior and connect those interior processes to things we see or experience on Earth's surface? This question is difficult to answer because geologists are unable to see deep inside Earth. However, geologists have found other ways to study the unseen interior of Earth. Their methods focus on two main types of **evidence**: direct evidence from rock samples and indirect evidence from seismic waves.

Academic Vocabulary

Suppose you think the air temperature is getting colder. Give two examples of evidence you could use to support your idea.

....

....

....

....

....

....

Rock Hitchhikers

Figure 1 These yellowish-green pieces of rock are *xenoliths*, from ancient Greek words *xeno*, meaning "foreign," and *lith*, meaning "rock." These xenoliths are fragments of peridotite, a rock that forms at least 50 to 60 kilometers deep inside Earth. They were picked up and carried to the surface by melted rock that later hardened and formed the grayish surrounding rock.

INTERACTIVITY

Explore how to investigate something you cannot directly observe.

Evidence From Rock Samples

Geologists have drilled holes as deep as 12.3 kilometers into Earth. Drilling brings up many samples of rock and gives geologists many clues. They learn about Earth's structure and conditions deep inside Earth where the rocks are formed. In addition, volcanoes sometimes carry rocks to the surface from depths of more than 100 kilometers. These rocks provide more information about Earth's interior, including clues about how matter and energy flow there. Some rocks from mountain ranges show evidence that they formed deep within Earth's crust and later were elevated as mountains formed. Also, in laboratories, geologists have used models to recreate conditions similar to those inside Earth to see how those conditions affect rock.

Evidence From Seismic Waves

To study Earth's interior, geologists also use an indirect method. When earthquakes occur, they produce **seismic waves** (SIZE mik). Geologists record the seismic waves and study how they travel through Earth. The paths of seismic waves reveal where the makeup or form of the rocks change, as shown in **Figure 2**.

Waves

Figure 2 Earthquakes produce different types of seismic waves that travel through Earth. The speed of these waves and the paths they take give geologists clues about the structure of the planet's interior.

Make Observations Compare and contrast the paths that P-waves and S-waves take through Earth. How do you think this information helps geologists understand Earth's interior?

the thickness of each layer.

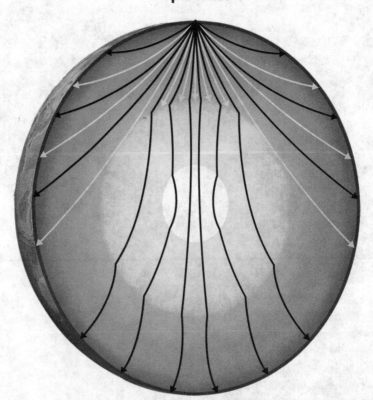

Earthquake epicenter

→ P-waves travel through solids and liquids.
→ S-waves only travel through solids.

Earth's Layers

After many years of research, scientists today know that Earth's interior is made up of three main layers: crust, mantle, and core. These layers vary greatly in thickness, composition, temperature, and pressure.

Pressure results from a force pressing on an area. Within Earth's interior, the mass of rock that is pressing down from above causes an increase of pressure on the rocks below. The deeper inside Earth's interior, the greater the pressure becomes. Pressure inside Earth increases much like water pressure in the swimming pool increases as you dive down deeper, as in **Figure 3**.

The temperature inside Earth increases as depth increases. Just beneath Earth's surface, the surrounding rock is cool. At about 20 meters down, the rock starts to get warmer. For every 40 meters of depth from that point, the temperature typically rises 1 degree Celsius. The rapid rise in temperature continues for several tens of kilometers. Eventually, the temperature increases more slowly, but steadily. The high temperatures inside Earth are mostly the result of the release of energy from radioactive substances and heat left over from the formation of Earth 4.6 billion years ago.

Pressure and Depth

Figure 3 The deeper that the swimmer goes, the greater the pressure on the swimmer from the surrounding water.

1. **Compare and Contrast** How is the water in the swimming pool similar to Earth's interior? How is it different? (*Hint:* Consider both temperature and pressure in your answer.)

   the deeper you go the more pressure. the water gets a lot colder the deeper you dive.

2. **CCC Use Proportional Relationships**
   At what location in the pool would the water pressure be greatest?

   the deep end

Pressure Increases

51

Earth's Layers

Figure 4 The crust and uppermost mantle make up the rigid lithosphere. The lithosphere rests on the softer material of the asthenosphere.

Translate Information Use the diagram to identify the layers and contrast how rigid they are.

Oceanic crust   Continental crust

Upper mantle

Depth (km)
0
-100
-200
-300
-350

Layer:
crust
Strength:
....

Layer:
Mantle
Strength:
....

2811–2886 km

2258 km   1222 km

The Crust Have you ever hiked up a mountain, toured a mine, or explored a cave? During each of these activities people interact with Earth's **crust**, the rock that forms Earth's outer layer. The crust is a layer of solid rock that includes both dry land and the ocean floor. The main **elements** of the rocks in the crust are oxygen and silicon.

The crust is much thinner than the layers beneath it. In most places, the crust is between 5 and 40 kilometers thick. It is thickest under high mountains, where it can be as thick as 80 kilometers, and it is thinnest beneath the ocean floor. There are two types of crust: oceanic crust and continental crust.

The crust that lies beneath the ocean is called oceanic crust. The composition of all oceanic crust is nearly the same. Its overall composition is much like basalt, with small amounts of ocean sediment on top. Basalt (buh SAWLT) is a dark, fine-grained rock.

Continental crust forms the continents. It contains many types of rocks. But overall the composition of continental crust is much like granite. Granite is a rock that usually is a light color and has coarse grains.

The Mantle Directly below the crust, the rock in Earth's interior changes. Rock here contains more magnesium and iron than does the rock above it. The rock below the crust is the solid material of the **mantle**, a layer of hot rock. Overall, the mantle is nearly 3,000 kilometers thick.

The uppermost part of the mantle is brittle rock, like the rock of the crust. Both the crust and the uppermost part of the mantle are strong, hard, and rigid. Geologists often group the crust and uppermost mantle into a single layer called the lithosphere. As shown in **Figure 4**, Earth's lithosphere is about 100 kilometers thick.

Below the lithosphere, the material is increasingly hotter. As a result, the part of the mantle just beneath the lithosphere is less rigid than the lithosphere itself. Over thousands of years, this part of the mantle may bend like a metal spoon, but it is still solid. This solid yet bendable layer is called the asthenosphere.

Beneath the asthenosphere is the lower mantle, which is hot, rigid, and under intense pressure. The lower mantle extends down to Earth's core.

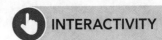

INTERACTIVITY

Examine the different layers of Earth.

Math Toolbox

Temperature in Earth's Layers

1. **Construct Graphs** 🖊 Use the data in the table to complete the line graph.

2. **Interpret Graphs** How does temperature change with depth in Earth's mantle?

   the closer you get to the core the hotter it gets

Depth (km)	Temperature (°C)
500	1,600°C
1,000	1,800°C
1,500	2,200°C
2,000	2,500°C
2,500	2,900°C

Temperature and Depth

Boundary between lithosphere and asthenosphere

Boundary between lower mantle and core

Temperature (°C): 4,000 — 3,000 — 2,000 — 1,000 — 16

Depth (km): 0 — 1,000 — 2,000 — 3,000

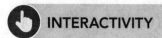

INTERACTIVITY

Analyze the heat of Earth's interior.

The Core Below the mantle is Earth's dense core. Earth's core occupies the center of the planet. It consists of two parts, a liquid outer core and a solid inner core. The outer core is 2,260 kilometers thick. The inner core is a solid ball with a radius of about 1,220 kilometers. Therefore, the total radius of the entire core is approximately 3,480 kilometers.

The **outer core** is a layer of molten metal surrounding the inner core. Despite enormous pressure, the outer core is liquid. The **inner core** is a dense ball of solid metal. In the inner core, extreme pressure squeezes the atoms of iron and nickel so much that they cannot spread out to become liquid despite the extremely high temperatures.

Currently, most evidence suggests that both parts of the core are mostly made of iron and nickel. Scientists have found data suggesting that the core also contains smaller amounts of oxygen, sulfur, and silicon.

Model It!

1. **SEP Evaluate Evidence** Label Earth's layers and use the text on the page to fill in the table with details about the layers.

$\frac{12}{12}$

	Thickness	Composition	Solid/Liquid
Crust:	10 – 80 km	Rocks	Solid
Mantle:	~~80 km~~ 2,880 km	Magma/Rock	Solid/liquid
Outer core:	2,260 km	Iron/nickle	liquid
Inner core:	1,220 km	Solid Iron/nickle	Solid
Total:	6,370 km		

2. **Compare and Contrast** Pick any two points inside Earth and label them A and B. Record their locations.

My Point A is in the ___upper Mantle___
My Point B is in the ___lower Mantle___

Compare and contrast Earth at those two points.

___high___ ___Bathin___ ___low___
___nutral___ ___Mantle___ ___hot___

_____

The Core and Earth's Magnetic Field

Scientists think that movements in the liquid outer core produce Earth's magnetic field. Earth's magnetic field affects the whole planet.

To understand how a magnetic field affects an object, think about a bar magnet. If you place the magnet on a piece of paper and sprinkle iron filings on the paper, the iron filings automatically line up in a pattern matching the bar's magnetic field. If you could surround Earth with iron filings, they would form a similar pattern. This is also what happens when you use a compass. The compass needle aligns with Earth's magnetic field.

READING CHECK **Identify Evidence** How can iron filings provide evidence that a bar magnet has a magnetic field?

iron is magnetic

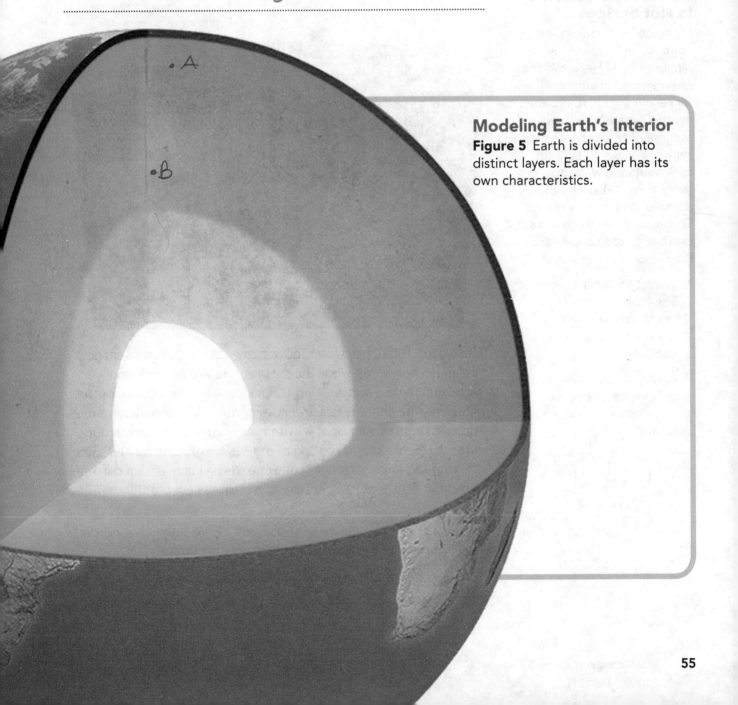

Modeling Earth's Interior
Figure 5 Earth is divided into distinct layers. Each layer has its own characteristics.

55

Movement in Earth's Mantle

Recall that Earth's mantle and core are extremely hot. Heat is a form of energy that flows. It transfers from matter at a higher temperature to matter at a lower temperature. The transfer of heat in the mantle drives a process called convection. This process is how matter and energy cycle through Earth's interior as well as its surface.

Convection Currents When you heat water on a stove, the water at the bottom of the pot gets hot and expands. As the heated water expands, its density decreases. Less-dense fluids flow up through denser fluids.

Convection Currents in Hot Springs

Figure 6 Hot springs are common in Yellowstone National Park. Here, melted snow and rainwater seep far below the crust into the mantle, where a shallow magma chamber heats the rock of Earth's crust. The rock heats the water to more than 200°C and puts it under very high pressure. This superheated groundwater rises to the surface and forms pools of hot water.

1. **Compare and Contrast** The heated water is (more/less) dense than the melted snow and rainwater.

2. **Apply Concepts** What process causes convection currents to form in a hot spring?

Less Dense Fluid flow threw as it heats up

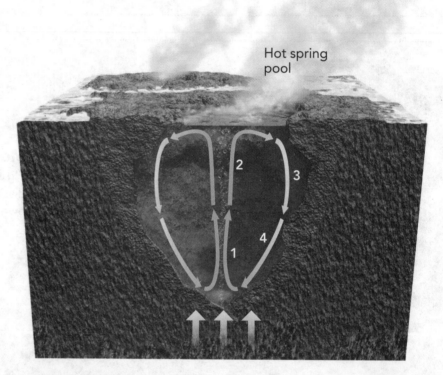

Hot spring pool

The warm, less dense water moves upward and floats over the cooler, denser water. Near the surface, the warm water cools, becoming denser again. It sinks back down to the bottom of the pot. Here, the water heats and rises again. The flows shown in **Figure 6** that transfer heat within matter are called convection currents. Heating and cooling of matter, changes in matter's density, and the force of gravity combine and set convection currents in motion. Without heat, convection currents eventually stop.

✅ **READING CHECK Cause and Effect** What three processes or forces combine to set convection currents in motion?

Convection Currents in Earth

Heat from the core and from the mantle itself drives convection currents. These currents carry hot, solid rock of the mantle outward and cooled, solid rock inward in a never-ending cycle.

As the oceanic lithosphere cools and sinks, it drives a pattern of mantle convection. The cold lithosphere moves down into the mantle, where it is heated. An upward return flow of hot rock completes the cycle, as shown in **Figure 7**. Over and over, the cycle of sinking and rising takes place. One full cycle takes millions of years. Convection currents are involved in the production of new rock at Earth's surface. There are also convection currents in the outer core.

ocean

crust

mantle

convection currents

Temperature: _hotter_
Density: _Less dense_
The Rock: _sinks_

Temperature: _colder_
Density: _More dense_
The Rock: _rises_

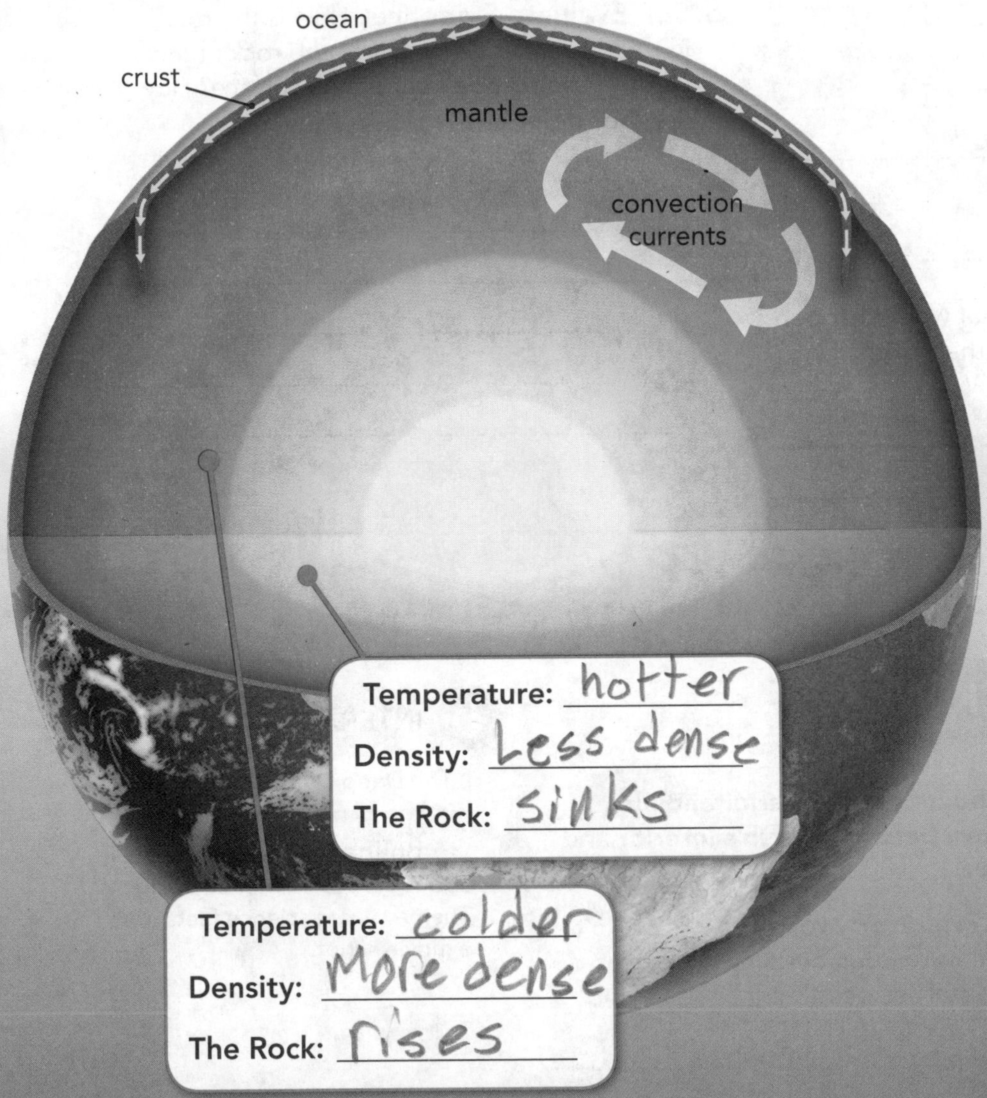

Mantle Convection

Figure 7 Complete the model by drawing the missing convection currents.

SEP Use Models Then complete the figure labels by using the terms in the box.

hotter

colder

less dense

more dense

sinks

rises

Make Meaning How can a solid such as mantle rock flow? Think about candle wax. In your science notebook, describe how you can make candle wax flow. What other solids have you observed that can flow?

MS-ESS2-1

1. **Identify** Name each layer of Earth, starting from Earth's center.

....

....

....

....

2. **Apply Concepts** Give examples of direct evidence and indirect evidence that geologists use to learn about Earth's interior.

....

....

....

....

....

3. **CCC Cause and Effect** What would happen to the convection currents in the mantle if Earth's interior cooled down? Why?

....

....

....

4. **SEP Construct Explanations** How does convection cause movement of material and energy in Earth's interior?

....

....

....

....

....

....

5. **SEP Evaluate Evidence** How is the rock in the deep mantle similar to the rock in the parts of the mantle nearest the surface? How are they different?

....

....

....

....

....

....

Quest CHECK-IN

In this lesson, you learned about Earth's interior and also how energy and material move between Earth's interior and its surface.

SEP Engage in Argument Explain why you think it is or isn't important for science fiction films to depict natural processes and geological events as accurately as possible.

....

....

....

....

👆 INTERACTIVITY

The Deep Drill

Go online to find out more about Earth's interior structure. Then evaluate science facts in a movie script.

INTERACTIVITY

Design a satellite that can collect electromagnetic field data.

Examining **Earth's Interior** *from* **Space**

How can you study Earth's interior? You engineer it! Geologist use satellites to help them visualize what they cannot see.

The Challenge: To understand how scientists study what they can't observe directly.

Phenomenon As Earth rotates, its liquid outer core spins. The flow and movement of Earth's oceans also create electric currents that generate secondary magnetic fields. Scientists call this process "motional induction." The European Space Agency (ESA) has launched three satellites into Earth's orbit that are sensitive to these electric currents.

The satellites also tell us many details about the electrical conductivity inside Earth's core—both the liquid of the outer core and the solid metallic sphere found at the center of the planet. A rock's ability to conduct electricity is related to its temperature, mineral composition, and water content. A satellite cannot directly measure these things. However, scientists can now draw reasonable conclusions about them by studying satellite data about the electric currents that flow through and just below Earth's surface.

Swarm Satellites launched in November 2013. The ESA's three-satellite Swarm mission is helping to improve our understanding of Earth's interior by taking measurements of its magnetic fields.

DESIGN CHALLENGE

Can you design your own satellite? Go to the Engineering Design Notebook to find out!

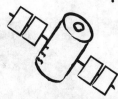

2 Minerals

Guiding Questions

- What are the characteristics and properties of minerals?
- What processes result in the formation of minerals?
- What processes explain the distribution of mineral resources on Earth?

Connections

Literacy Integrate With Visuals

Math Calculate

MS-ESS2-1, MS-ESS3-1

HANDS-ON LAB

ʊInvestigate Model mineral crystals and observe how they can change.

Vocabulary

mineral
crystal
crystallization

Academic Vocabulary

organic

Connect It!

✎ **Circle two crystals in the photo.**

Relate Change Do you think these crystals formed in conditions that were stable or that changed often? Explain.

....

....

....

....

Defining Minerals

Look at the objects in **Figure 1**. They are solid matter that formed deep beneath Earth's surface. They are beautiful, gigantic crystals of the mineral selenite, which is a form of gypsum. But what is a mineral?

Characteristics
A **mineral** is a naturally occurring solid that can form by inorganic processes and has a crystal structure and definite chemical composition. For a substance to be a mineral, it must have the following five characteristics.

Naturally Occurring
All minerals are substances that form by natural processes. Gypsum forms naturally from chemical elements that precipitate from water.

Solid
A mineral is always a solid, which means it has a definite volume and shape. The particles in a solid are packed tightly together. Gypsum is a solid.

Forms by Inorganic Processes
All minerals must form by inorganic processes. That is, they can form from materials that were not a part of living things. Gypsum forms naturally as sulfate-rich solutions evaporate. Some minerals, such as calcite, form from both inorganic and organic processes.

Crystal Structure
The particles of a mineral line up in a pattern that repeats over and over again. The repeating pattern of a mineral's particles forms a solid called a **crystal**. The gypsum in the image has a crystal structure.

Definite Chemical Composition
A mineral has a definite chemical composition. This means it always contains the same elements in certain proportions. Gypsum always contains calcium, oxygen, sulfur, and hydrogen, in set proportions.

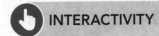

INTERACTIVITY

Explain what the term *mineral* means to you.

Reflect Write down where you have heard of minerals before, and the names of any minerals that play a role in your everyday life.

Mineral Giants
Figure 1 Dwarfed by megacrystals of the mineral selenite, miners explore Mexico's Cave of Crystals. Located about 300 meters below Earth's surface, the cave contains some of the largest crystals ever discovered in nature—up to 12 meters long!

Mineral Properties

Geologists have identified and named more than 5,000 minerals, though only about 20 make up most of the rocks of Earth's crust. Because there are so many minerals, telling them apart can be challenging. Each mineral has characteristic properties that are used to identify and describe it. **Figure 2** shows some of the properties of the mineral pyrite.

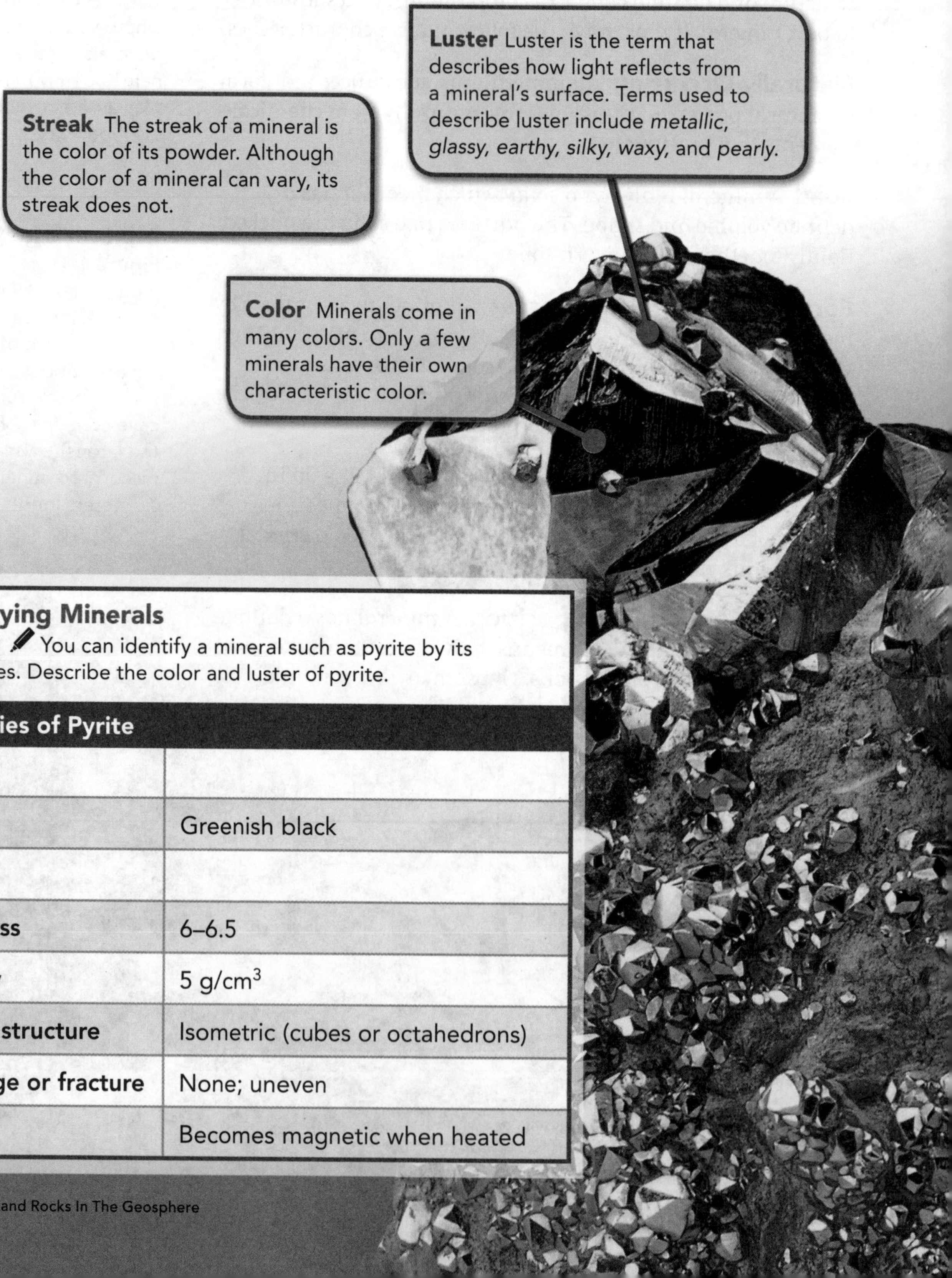

Luster Luster is the term that describes how light reflects from a mineral's surface. Terms used to describe luster include *metallic, glassy, earthy, silky, waxy,* and *pearly.*

Streak The streak of a mineral is the color of its powder. Although the color of a mineral can vary, its streak does not.

Color Minerals come in many colors. Only a few minerals have their own characteristic color.

Identifying Minerals

Figure 2 ✏️ You can identify a mineral such as pyrite by its properties. Describe the color and luster of pyrite.

Properties of Pyrite	
Color	
Streak	Greenish black
Luster	
Hardness	6–6.5
Density	5 g/cm^3
Crystal structure	Isometric (cubes or octahedrons)
Cleavage or fracture	None; uneven
Special	Becomes magnetic when heated

Density Each mineral has a characteristic density, or mass in a given volume. To calculate a mineral's density, use this formula: Density = Mass/Volume

Cleavage and Fracture A mineral that splits easily along flat surfaces has the property called cleavage. Whether a mineral has cleavage depends on how the atoms in its crystals are arranged. Most minerals do not split apart evenly. Instead, they have a characteristic type of fracture. Fracture describes how a mineral looks when it breaks apart in an irregular way.

Special Properties Some minerals can be identified by special physical properties. For example, calcite bends light to produce double images. Other minerals conduct electricity, glow when placed under ultraviolet light, or are magnetic.

Crystal Structure All the crystals of a mineral have the same crystal structure. Different minerals have crystals that are shaped differently. Geologists classify crystals by the number of faces, or sides, on the crystal and the angles at which the faces meet.

Math Toolbox

Calculate Density

A sample of the mineral cinnabar has a mass of 251.1 g and a volume of 31.0 cm^3.

SEP Use Mathematics What is the density of cinnabar?

....

....

....

....

Hardness The Mohs hardness scale is used to rank the hardness of minerals from 1 being the softest to 10 being the hardest. A mineral can scratch any mineral softer than itself but can be scratched by any mineral that is harder.

Where Minerals Form

Figure 3 ✏ Minerals can form by crystallization of magma and lava or precipitation of materials dissolved in water. Circle the area where you might find a cave with crystals similar to the large crystals shown in **Figure 1**.

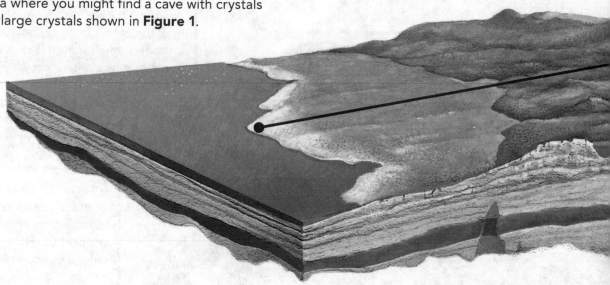

HANDS-ON LAB

⬛**Investigate** Model mineral crystals and observe how they can change.

Academic Vocabulary

You might be familiar with term *organic food*. How does this meaning of *organic* differ from the scientific meaning?

....

....

....

....

....

Mineral Formation

In general, minerals can form in a few different ways and at different locations at or below Earth's surface. Some minerals form from organic processes. Other minerals form from the materials dissolved in evaporating solutions of water. Many minerals form when magma and lava originally heated by the energy of Earth's interior cool and solidify. Finally, some minerals form when other minerals are heated or compressed, which causes the material to deform.

Organic Minerals
All minerals can form by inorganic processes. However, many **organic** processes can also form minerals. For instance, animals such as cows and humans produce skeletons made of the mineral calcium phosphate. Ultimately, the energy used to drive the processes of mineral formation in most living things can be traced all the way back to the sun and the plants that use its energy.

Minerals From Solutions
Sometimes the elements and compounds that form minerals dissolve in water and form solutions. On Earth's surface, energy from the sun can cause water to evaporate, leaving behind minerals. Water below Earth's surface, which is under intense pressure and at high temperatures, can pick up elements and compounds from surrounding rock. When these elements and compounds leave the water solution through precipitation, crystallization can occur.

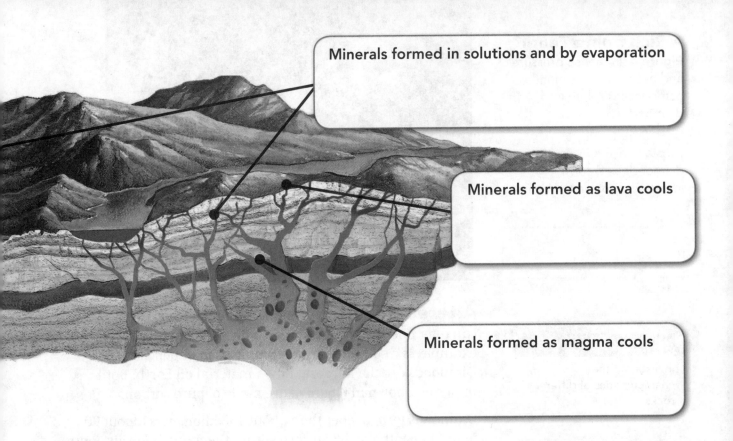

Minerals formed in solutions and by evaporation

Minerals formed as lava cools

Minerals formed as magma cools

Crystallization is the process by which atoms are arranged to form a material that has a crystal structure. Minerals such as halite, calcite, and gypsum form through crystallization when bodies of water on Earth's surface evaporate.

In another example, the huge crystals in **Figure 1** formed from a solution of water heated by energy from Earth's interior that eventually cooled underground. But the process was an extremely long one, taking place over millions of years.

Minerals From Magma and Lava

Many minerals form when hot magma from Earth's interior cools higher up in the crust, or as lava cools and hardens on the surface. When these liquids cool to a solid state, they form crystals.

The size of the crystals depends on several factors, including the rate at which the melted rock cools. Slow cooling leads to the formation of large crystals, such as coarse quartz and feldspar crystals found in granite that slowly cools underground. Fast cooling leaves very little time for crystals to grow. Lava cools quickly on the surface or under water and forms small crystals, such as pyroxene and fine-grained olivine in basalt rock of the oceanic crust.

☑ READING CHECK **Summarize Text** What type of minerals might a geologist expect to find near the site of an ancient lava flow? Explain.

....

....

Literacy Connection

Integrate With Visuals
Underline the name of each mineral mentioned on this page. Then, record each mineral in its correct place in **Figure 3**.

A Ring from a Pencil?

Figure 4 Immense pressure and heat in Earth's mantle compacts graphite into diamond.

SEP Construct Explanations Why do diamonds only form in certain spots in the mantle?

....

....

....

graphite

cut diamond

 INTERACTIVITY

Investigate the characteristics of different rocks.

Altered Minerals A change of temperature or pressure can alter one mineral into a new mineral. Graphite, for example, is a soft mineral commonly used in pencils. Diamonds are the hardest known material on Earth. Both minerals, shown in **Figure 4**, are made of pure carbon.

Diamonds form deeper than about 150 kilometers (about 90 miles) beneath Earth's surface within the mantle. At this depth below continental crust, temperatures reach between 900°C to 1,300°C, and the pressure is about 50,000 times greater than at Earth's surface. The intense pressure and high temperature alter the structure of the carbon atoms in graphite, forming diamond.

These diamond zones may also contain magma. Long ago, the pressure that formed diamonds also caused magma to squeeze toward Earth's surface, where it might erupt. Sometimes, diamonds were carried along for the ride. When the magma cooled in pipe-like formations, the diamonds were embedded in this rock.

Model It

Diamond Formation

SEP Develop Models Use the information in the text and **Figure 3** to draw a diagram that shows how diamonds form. Your model should show and label the following parts of the process:

1. Graphite in the mantle that is under intense pressure becomes diamonds.

2. In the past, magma from the mantle moved quickly toward Earth's surface, forming pipes.

3. The magma cooled with the diamonds trapped within it.

Mineral Distribution

The common minerals that make up the rocks of Earth's crust are found abundantly throughout Earth's surface. Other minerals are much less common because their formation depends on certain materials and conditions that may be limited. Other minerals may form as the result of processes that take a very long time, which will limit where and how much of the mineral can form. The process by which diamonds are formed is one example.

Geological processes often tied to plate tectonics, such as volcanic eruptions or evaporations in ocean basins, can cause certain minerals to collect in concentrated deposits. These deposits, or ores, are mined for the valuable materials they contain. **Figure 5** shows the distribution of some of Earth's mineral resources.

INTERACTIVITY

Identify a mineral based on its characteristic properties.

✓ READING CHECK **Integrate With Visuals** What ideas from the text are illustrated in the map in **Figure 5**?

....

....

Mineral Resources

Figure 5 The map shows the location of some important mineral resources. Many of the minerals represented on the map are not evenly distributed across the planet.

SEP Construct Explanations What patterns do you notice in the distributions of different minerals on Earth?

....

....

....

....

....

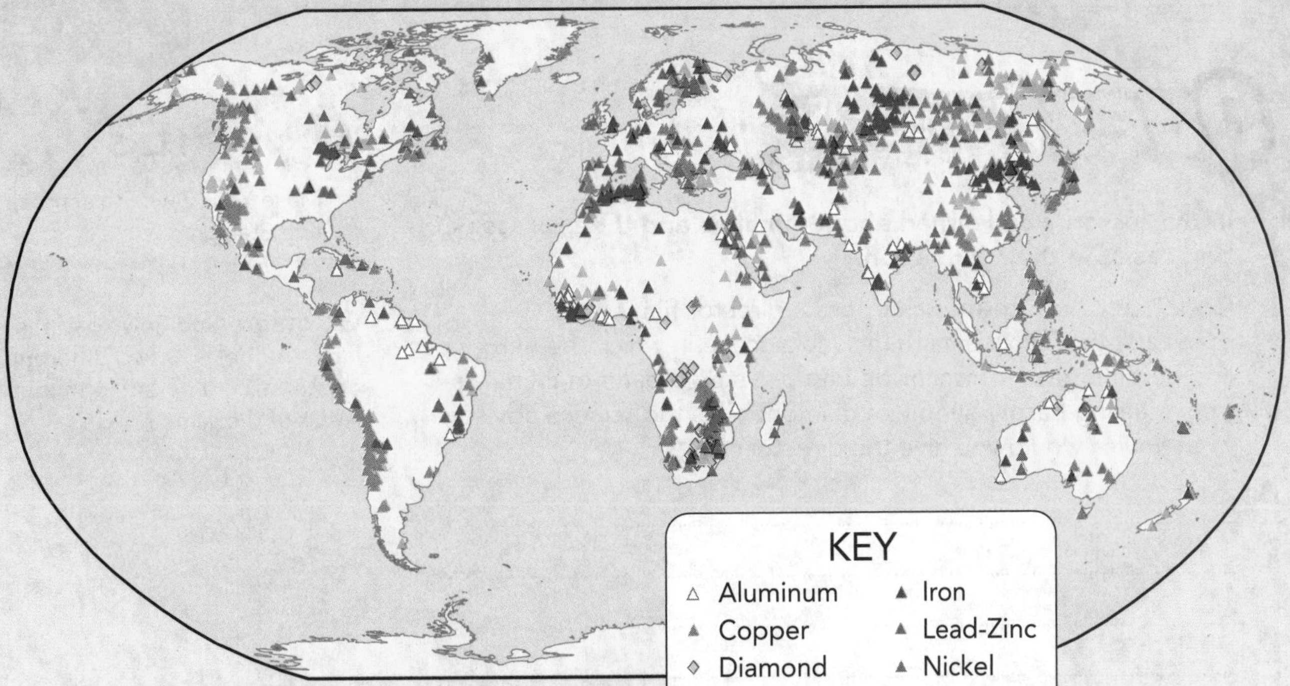

KEY

△ Aluminum   ▲ Iron
▲ Copper   ▲ Lead-Zinc
◇ Diamond   ▲ Nickel
▲ Gold

MS-ESS2-1, MS-ESS3-1

1. Analyze Properties What are some of the properties that geologists use to identify and describe minerals?

....

....

....

2. SEP Construct Explanations Why aren't diamonds found evenly distributed on Earth?

....

....

....

....

3. Apply Concepts Amber is a solid material used in jewelry. It forms in nature only by the process of pine tree resin hardening. Explain why you think amber is or is not a mineral.

....

....

....

....

4. CCC Cause and Effect What role does the sun's energy play in the formation of minerals from solutions?

....

....

....

....

....

5. SEP Develop Models 🖊 Draw a flow chart or cycle diagram to show one way a mineral gets recycled in nature and forms a new mineral.

Quest CHECK-INS

In this lesson, you learned about minerals and the processes that result in their formation.

Construct Arguments Suppose a director filming a science fiction film wants to include a scene in which the hero and heroine travel down inside Earth to stop a band of criminals from stealing Earth's supply of diamonds. As the science advisor, what advice would you give the director?

....

....

....

....

HANDS-ON LAB

Make Your Own Stalactites and Stalagmites

Go online and download the lab to model how two different crystal structures can form as a result of the same process.

MS-ESS2-1

The Cost of
TECHNOLOGY

Coltan ore before processing to extract tantalum.

You may never have heard of the element tantalum, but you probably use it every day. The electrical properties of tantalum make it a good material to use in capacitors in electronic devices. And it's found in all the smartphones, laptops, and other electronics that billions of people use to stay organized, get work done, and communicate with each other.

Tantalum must be extracted from an ore called coltan. The ore must be mined and refined before the tantalum can be used. By the turn of the 21st century, worldwide demand for electronics reached a peak, which increased demand for tantalum. Prior to 2000, most of the world's tantalum was extracted from coltan mined in Australia and Brazil. These countries have stricter mining regulations, which increases the cost of mining tantalum.

When demand for tantalum exploded, coltan mining increased in the Democratic Republic of Congo (DRC) and neighboring countries in Africa. But the DRC has been torn apart by civil war, which has lured armed coltan miners looking for a fast profit. The government does little to regulate how the coltan is mined. The unregulated, often illegal, mining provides inexpensive tantalum but destroys vital wildlife habitats and helps to fund continued conflict in this war-ravaged country.

MY COMMUNITY

How would you solve the problem of the need for coltan versus the need to source the coltan responsibly? Work in a small group to identify possible solutions. Conduct internet research to find facts and evidence that support your arguments.

These miners search for coltan, iron ore, and manganese at the Mudere mine in eastern Democratic Republic of Congo.

(3) Rocks

Guiding Questions

- What are the three major types of rocks and how do they form?
- How is the formation of rocks the result of the flow of energy and cycling of matter within Earth?

Connections

Literacy Summarize Text

Math Analyze Relationships

MS-ESS2-1

HANDS-ON LAB

uInvestigate Examine how pressure can change rock.

Vocabulary

igneous rock
sedimentary rock
sediment
metamorphic
  rock

Academic Vocabulary

apply

Connect It!

✏ **Draw an outline of what the weathered rock may have looked like 2,000 years ago.**

SEP Construct Explanations How do you think the rock formation will continue to change over time?

....

....

....

....

....

Describing Rocks

In southern Utah, spires and buttes of red sandstone rise up into the sky in Monument Valley (**Figure 1**). To a tourist or other casual observer, these rock formations seem to stand motionless and unchanging. But every moment of every day, forces are at work on these rocks, slowly changing their shapes and sizes. Weathering, erosion, transportation, and deposition all work to wear away and alter the appearance of the rock formations.

Rocks, like the sandstone in Monument Valley, are made of mixtures of minerals and other materials. To describe rocks, geologists observe mineral composition, color, and texture.

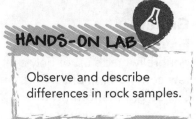

HANDS-ON LAB

Observe and describe differences in rock samples.

Towers of Rock

Figure 1 The striking red color of Monument Valley is the result of iron oxide minerals exposed within the rock.

Granite

Figure 2 Granite is generally made up of only a few common minerals. This coarse granite formed when magma cooled slowly.

1. Claim ✏️ Circle the best word to complete each sentence.

Granite is generally (dark/light) in color.

Granite has a (high/low) silica content.

The grains in granite are (fine/coarse).

2. Evidence What evidence did you use to make your claim?

....

....

3. Reasoning Explain how your evidence supported your claim.

....

....

....

....

....

....

Mica

Quartz

Granite

Feldspar

Hornblende

Mineral Composition and Color Some rocks contain only a single mineral. Other rocks contain several minerals. About 20 minerals make up most of the rocks of Earth's crust. These minerals are known as rock-forming minerals.

A rock's color provides clues to the rock's mineral composition. Granite, as shown in **Figure 2**, is generally a light-colored rock that has high silica content, meaning it is rich in the elements silicon and oxygen.

Texture Most rocks are made up of particles of minerals or other rocks, which geologists call grains. To describe the texture of a rock, geologists use terms that are based on the size, shape, and pattern of the grains. For example, rocks with grains that are large and easy to see are coarse-grained. In fine-grained rocks, grains can be seen only with a microscope.

Origin Using mineral composition, color, and texture, geologists classify a rock's origin—how the rock formed. Geologists have classified rocks into three major groups based on origin: igneous rock, sedimentary rock, and metamorphic rock.

✅ **READING CHECK** **Determine Meaning** *Ignis* means "fire" in Latin. What is "fiery" about igneous rocks?

INTERACTIVITY

Identify and evaluate the characteristics of different rocks.

Plan It!

Rocky Observations

As part of a geological investigation you are conducting, you observe three rock samples.

SEP Analyze Data What characteristics would you examine to help you distinguish among the three rocks?

....

....

How Rocks Form

Each type of rock, whether its igneous, sedimentary, or metamorphic, forms in a different way.

Igneous Rock Rock that forms from cooled magma or lava is **igneous rock** (IG nee us). Igneous rocks can look very different from each other. The temperature and composition of the molten rock determine the kind of igneous rock that is formed.

Igneous rock may form on or beneath Earth's surface from molten material that cools and hardens. Extrusive rock is igneous rock formed from lava that erupted onto Earth's surface. Basalt is the most common extrusive rock, making up a large part of oceanic crust. Igneous rock that formed when magma hardened beneath the surface of Earth is called intrusive rock. The most abundant type of intrusive rock in the continental crust is granite. Granite forms tens of kilometers below Earth's surface and over hundreds of thousands of years or longer. When granite ends up close to the surface, it may be mined for use as road-building material, in a crushed state, or as a building material, in large polished slabs.

The texture of most igneous rock depends on the size and shape of its mineral crystals (**Figure 3**). Rapidly cooling lava found at or near Earth's surface forms fine-grained igneous rocks with small crystals or no minerals at all. Slowly cooling magma below Earth's surface forms coarse-grained rocks, such as granite and diorite, with large crystals. Intrusive rocks have larger grains than extrusive rocks. Extrusive rocks that cool too quickly to form any minerals are called glass.

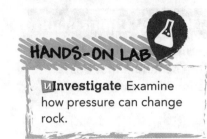

HANDS-ON LAB

и**Investigate** Examine how pressure can change rock.

Igneous Rock Formation

Figure 3 The texture of igneous rock varies according to how it forms.

SEP Evaluate Evidence ✏ Did the rocks in the photographs form at A or B? Write your answers in the spaces provided.

Diorite
A very coarse-grained, intrusive igneous rock. ....

Rhyolite
Rhyolite is a fine-grained, extrusive igneous rock with a composition that is similar to granite. ....

73

Summarize Text Underline the sentence that best summarizes the paragraph.

Sedimentary Rock

Most **sedimentary rock** (sed uh MEN tur ee) forms when small particles of rocks or the remains of plants and animals are pressed and cemented together. The raw material is **sediment**—small, solid pieces of material that come from rocks or living things. As shown in **Figure 4**, sediment forms and becomes sedimentary rock through a sequence of processes: weathering and erosion, transportation, deposition, compaction, and cementation. Examples of sedimentary rock include sandstone, shale, and limestone.

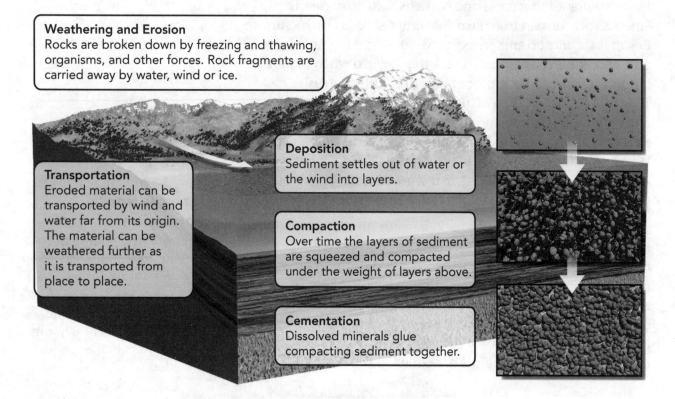

Weathering and Erosion
Rocks are broken down by freezing and thawing, organisms, and other forces. Rock fragments are carried away by water, wind or ice.

Deposition
Sediment settles out of water or the wind into layers.

Transportation
Eroded material can be transported by wind and water far from its origin. The material can be weathered further as it is transported from place to place.

Compaction
Over time the layers of sediment are squeezed and compacted under the weight of layers above.

Cementation
Dissolved minerals glue compacting sediment together.

Sequencing Sedimentary Rock Formation

Figure 4 Sedimentary rock forms in layers that are then buried below the surface. Formation occurs through a series of processes over millions of years.

1. **CCC Patterns** ✎ Summarize how sedimentary rock forms by using the flow chart to sequence the following processes correctly: *transportation, compaction, cementation, weathering and erosion,* and *deposition*.

2. **Synthesize Information** Which two processes turn layers of loose sediment into hard sedimentary rock?

....

....

Metamorphic Rock

Metamorphic rock (met uh MOR fik) forms when a rock is changed by heat or pressure or by chemical reactions. When high heat and pressure are **applied** to rock, the rock's shape, texture, or composition can change, as shown in **Figure 5**.

Most metamorphic rock forms deep inside Earth, where both heat and pressure are much greater than at Earth's surface. Collisions between Earth's plates can push rock down toward the deeper, hotter mantle, altering the rock. The heat that changes rock into metamorphic rock can also come from very hot magma that rises up into colder rock. The high heat of this magma changes surrounding rock into metamorphic rock.

Very high pressure can also change rock into metamorphic rock. When plates collide, or when rock is buried deep beneath millions of tons of rock, the pressure can be enough to chemically change the rock's minerals to other types. The physical appearance, texture, and crystal structure of the minerals changes as a result.

Metamorphic rocks whose grains are arranged in parallel layers or bands are said to be foliated. For example, the crystals in granite can be flattened to form the foliated texture of gneiss. Some metamorphic rocks, such as marble, are nonfoliated. Their mineral grains are arranged randomly.

✅ **READING CHECK Summarize Text** Explain the basic difference between igneous and metamorphic rock.

....

....

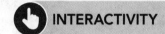 **INTERACTIVITY**

Explore different regions' rocks.

Granite

Heat and Pressure

Gneiss

Marble

Heat and Pressure

Limestone

Metamorphic Changes
Figure 5 🖉 Heat and pressure can change one type of rock into another. Label each rock *sedimentary*, *igneous*, or *metamorphic*. Indicate whether the metamorphic rocks are foliated. Then shade the correct arrowhead to show which rock can form from the other rock.

Eruption!

Figure 6 A volcanic eruption brings up magma that will be subject to weathering and erosion when it cools.

Evaluate Change Would you describe the processes that change the rocks making up this volcano as fast or slow? Explain.

....

....

....

....

....

The Flow of Energy

No matter what type of rock is formed, it formed as a result of the energy that flows through the Earth system. The energy that drives forces affecting the formation of sedimentary rock, such as weathering, erosion, transportation, and deposition, comes in the form of heat from the sun. Heat from Earth's interior drives the processes that control the formation of igneous and metamorphic rocks.

READING CHECK **Summarize Text** What are the sources of energy that drive volcanic processes?

....

....

....

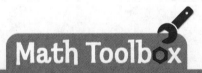

Math Toolbox

Pressure and Depth

Pressure increases inside Earth as depth increases.

1. **SEP Interpret Data** About how far must one travel to experience the greatest pressure inside Earth?

....

2. **Analyze Relationships** How is pressure related to depth?

....

....

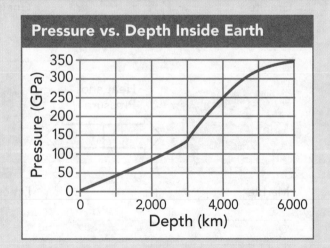

Pressure vs. Depth Inside Earth

☑ LESSON 3 Check

MS-ESS2-1

1. Identify What are the three major kinds of rocks?

....

....

2. CCC Cause and Effect What is the source of energy that drives the weathering and erosion of sedimentary rock? Explain.

....

....

....

....

3. SEP Evaluate Evidence High heat melts a deposit of sedimentary rock, which then hardens into new rock. What kind of rock forms? Explain your answer.

....

....

....

....

....

4. Analyze Properties You are examining a sample of igneous rock. What factors affect the kind of igneous rock found in the sample?

....

....

....

....

....

5. SEP Construct Explanations If rocks, such as the sandstone formations in **Figure 1**, are constantly changing as a result of weathering and erosion, then why do they appear to be stable and unchanging to us?

....

....

....

....

....

....

....

....

Quest CHECK-IN

In this lesson, you learned about rocks and how energy from the sun and Earth's interior drives their formation.

SEP Use Models How could the formation of metamorphic rock be modeled in a science fiction film through special effects?

....

....

....

....

....

👆 INTERACTIVITY

Rocky Business

Go online to evaluate the science facts in a movie script and the ways they are presented, revising the script as necessary.

4 Cycling of Rocks

Guiding Questions

- How are Earth's materials cycled in the rock cycle?
- How does the flow of energy drive the processes of the rock cycle?

Connection

Literacy Translate Information

MS-ESS2-1

HANDS-ON LAB

uInvestigate Determine the relative ages of rocks.

Vocabulary

rock cycle

Academic Vocabulary

process
source

Connect It!

✏ **Look closely at the desert photograph in Figure 1. Circle a change that you can observe in the image.**

Examine Change What change did you observe? What agent is causing the change?

....

....

Relate Change What rock-forming processes are taking place?

....

....

The Cycling of Earth's Materials

The rock in Earth's crust is always changing. Forces deep inside Earth and at the surface build, destroy, and change the rocks in the crust. The **rock cycle** is the series of processes that occur on Earth's surface and in the crust and mantle that slowly change rocks from one kind to another. For example, the **process** of weathering breaks down granite into sediment that gets carried away and dropped by the wind. Some of that sediment can later form sandstone.

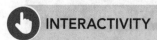

INTERACTIVITY

Explore the different phases of the rock cycle.

Academic Vocabulary

Circle the name of a process in the text. Then name two processes you go through in your daily life.

....

Rock Cycle in Action

Figure 1 In Death Valley, California, and other locations on Earth's surface, processes of the rock cycle continuously move and change sediment and rocks.

HANDS-ON LAB

☑**Investigate** Determine the relative ages of rocks.

Translate Information

Review the sequence of events described in the text. Then number the materials from Granite Mountain in the order in which they move through the rock cycle.

Sandstone ....

Granite ....

Quartzite ....

Sediment ....

Granite Mountain

Figure 2 Processes in the rock cycle change the granite in Granite Mountain.

SEP Evidence Circle the words that best complete the sentences.

The (leaves/roots) of the trees on the mountain cause (weathering/erosion) of the granite. (Erosion/Deposition) by streams transports sediment away.

Reason Quantitatively How long will it most likely take for processes in the rock cycle to change most of Granite Mountain into sediment? Check the box next to the correct answer.

☐ less than 1 million years
☐ 1 million years
☐ 10 million years or more

The Flow of Energy in the Rock Cycle

There are many pathways by which rocks move through the rock cycle. These pathways and the processes and events they include are patterns that repeat again and again. For example, **Figure 2** shows Granite Mountain in Arizona. The granite in Granite Mountain formed millions of years ago below Earth's surface as magma cooled.

After the granite formed, the forces of mountain building slowly pushed the granite up to the surface. Since then, weathering and erosion have been breaking down and carrying away the granite. Transportation by streams carries some of the pieces of granite, called sediment, to rivers and eventually to the ocean. What might happen next?

Over millions of years, layers of sediment build up on the ocean floor. Slowly, the weight of the layers would physically compact the sediment. Then calcite that is dissolved in the ocean water could cement the particles together, causing a chemical change in the material. Over time, the material that once formed the igneous rock granite of Granite Mountain could become the sedimentary rock sandstone.

Sediment could keep piling up and burying the sandstone. The motion of Earth's plates could move the sandstone even deeper below the surface. Eventually, extreme pressure could deform the rocks by compacting them and causing physical and chemical changes in the rock particles. Some of the particles might crystallize. Silica, the main ingredient in quartz, would replace the calcite cement. The rock's physical texture would change from gritty to smooth. After millions of years, the sandstone could change into the metamorphic rock quartzite. Or, the heat below Earth's surface could melt the sandstone and form magma, starting the cycle over again. **Figure 3** shows this process.

The Rock Cycle

Figure 3 Patterns of repeating events in the rock cycle, including melting, weathering, erosion, and the application of heat and pressure, constantly change rocks from one type into another type. Through these events, Earth's materials get recycled.

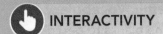
INTERACTIVITY

Have an interactive look at the rock cycle.

1. **SEP Develop Models** ✏ Study the photographs of the Earth materials. Fill in each blank box in the rock cycle diagram with the correct material.

2. **SEP Use Models** ✏ Study the diagram. Then label each arrow with the correct term: *melting, weathering and erosion, heat and pressure, volcanic activity,* or *deposition.* (*Hint:* To fit your answers, abbreviate "weathering and erosion" as "w & e.")

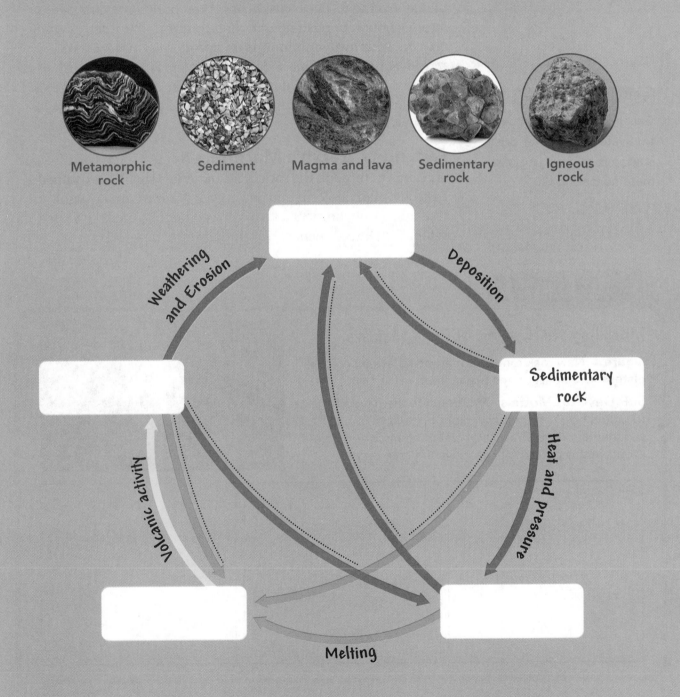

Academic Vocabulary

Fill in the blanks to describe two sources.

.... is the source of igneous rocks.

.... is the source of the energy my body needs.

☑ READING CHECK

Cause and Effect Underline the plate motion that can lead to rock changing into metamorphic rock.

Plate Tectonics and the Rock Cycle

The rock cycle is driven in part by plate tectonics. Recall that Earth's lithosphere is made up of huge plates that slowly move over Earth's surface due to convection currents in the mantle. As the plates move, they carry the continents and ocean floors with them. Plate movements help drive the rock cycle by helping to form magma, the **source** of igneous rock.

Where oceanic plates move apart, magma moves upward and fills the gap with new igneous rock. Where an oceanic plate moves beneath a continental plate, magma forms and rises. The result is a volcano where lava flows onto the overlying plate, forming igneous rock. Sedimentary rock can also result from plate movement. The collision of continental plates can be strong enough to push up a mountain range. Weathering and erosion wear away mountains and produce sediment that may eventually become sedimentary rock. Finally, a collision between continental plates can push rocks down deep beneath the surface. Here, heat and pressure could change the rocks to metamorphic rock.

Cycling of Earth's Materials

As the rock in Earth's crust moves through the rock cycle, material is not lost or gained. Instead it changes form and gets recycled. For example, basalt that forms from hardened lava can weather and erode to form sediment. The sediment can eventually form new rock.

Model It!

Modeling the Cycling of Rock Material

Figure 4 New rock forms from erupting lava where two plates move apart on the ocean floor.

SEP Develop Models ✏ Complete the diagram to model how rock material might cycle from lava to sedimentary rock. Draw and label three more possible events in this pattern of change in the rock cycle.

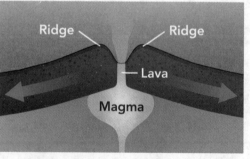

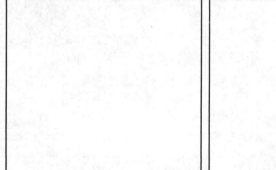
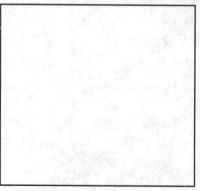
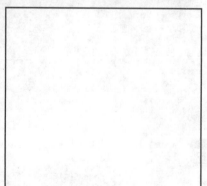

☑ LESSON 4 Check

MS-ESS2-1

1. **Relate Change** What processes can recycle sedimentary rock into sediment?

....

....

....

2. **CCC Describe Patterns** Describe a process that happens again and again in the rock cycle.

....

....

....

....

3. **SEP Construct Explanations** Explain why the change from metamorphic rock to magma almost always occurs below Earth's surface.

....

....

....

....

....

....

4. **SEP Evaluate Evidence** Do you think that plate tectonics plays a major or minor role in the rock cycle? Explain your answer.

....

....

....

....

....

....

Use the rock cycle diagram in Figure 3 to help you answer Question 5.

5. **SEP Use Models** Describe two different ways that sedimentary rock can become igneous rock.

....

....

....

....

....

....

....

Quest CHECK-IN

In this lesson, you learned how Earth's materials move through the rock cycle. You also learned about the flow of energy that drives the processes of the rock cycle.

SEP Ask Questions Suppose you could meet with a science consultant for movies and scripts. What questions would you have for the consultant about reviewing, evaluating, and revising scripts to make them more scientifically accurate?

....

....

....

👆 INTERACTIVITY

The Rock Cyclers

Go online to identify and evaluate scientific facts of the rock cycle in a movie script, and then revise the script to make it more accurate.

Mighty Mauna Loa

The high summit of Mauna Loa is often surrounded by tropical rain clouds. The large volcano, outlined in red on the satellite image below, makes up a majority of the area of the main island of Hawaii.

Mauna Loa is one of Hawaii's most active volcanoes, located on the largest of the islands. The volcano sits on an active hotspot. For more than 80 million years, the Hawaiian Islands and seamounts have formed as the Pacific Plate has been sliding northwest over a hotspot—a plume of magma that causes eruptions through the overlying plate.

Mauna Loa illustrates the rock cycle in action. Over time, rock will continue to be buried as more lava flows and more sediment is carried down the volcano. Under high temperatures and pressure, some of the sedimentary rock will become metamorphic rock.

When Mauna Loa erupts, magma from inside Earth pours out of the volcano as lava. The lava flows down the slopes of the volcano.

Lava cools to form igneous rock. Some lava cools on the slopes of the volcano. Other lava flows to the ocean, where the lava cools and slowly increases the size of the island.

Weathering and erosion break down some of the igneous rock. Through the process of deposition, some of this sediment is carried down the volcano. As the sediment becomes compacted, it forms sedimentary rock.

1. **SEP Develop Models**  Complete the diagram using arrows, labels, and captions to describe the processes that drive the rock cycle on Mauna Loa.

2. **CCC Patterns** The last few eruptions of Mauna Loa happened in 1942, 1949, 1950, 1975, and 1984. The volcano has erupted 33 times since 1843. When do you think the next eruption will occur, and why do you think so?

....

....

....

....

....

....

3. **SEP Construct Explanations** Why do you think Mauna Loa erupts periodically instead of steadily?

....

....

....

....

....

....

☑ TOPIC 2 Review and Assess

1 Earth's Interior

MS-ESS2-1

1. Which part(s) of Earth's interior has two distinct layers?

A. crust
B. mantle
C. core
D. crust and core

2. Which is Earth's thinnest layer?

A. crust
B. inner core
C. mantle
D. outer core

3. Which of the following is an example of indirect evidence about Earth's layers?

A. rock samples obtained by drilling
B. mantle rocks produced by volcanoes
C. changes observed in seismic wave data
D. data gathered from high–pressure lab experiments

4. Heat in the core and the .... cause

...., which help to cycle

material on Earth.

5. SEP Develop Models 🖊 Draw a model to show the flow of energy and rock material through convection currents in Earth's interior. Be sure to show movement, label the layers involved, and give your model a title.

2 Minerals

MS-ESS2-1

6. Which statement best identifies the substance whose characteristics are listed in the table?

Characteristic	Observation
Naturally occurring	Yes
Can form by inorganic processes	No
Solid	Yes
Crystal structure	No
Definite chemical composition	No

A. It is not a mineral because it is a solid.
B. It is a mineral because it occurs naturally.
C. It is not a mineral because it doesn't have a crystal structure.
D. It is a mineral because it forms only organically.

7. What causes the crystals in gneiss to line up in bands?

A. deposition
B. erosion
C. pressure
D. weathering

8. *Metallic, glassy, earthy,* and *pearly* are words that describe a mineral's ....

9. SEP Analyze Data Mineral A has a hardness of 5. Mineral B has a hardness of 7. Mineral C can scratch Mineral A, but it can be scratched by Mineral B. What ranking on the Mohs hardness scale should Mineral C be assigned? Explain.

....

....

....

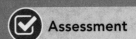
3 Rocks

MS-ESS2-1

10. Which process acts on Earth's surface to break rocks into pieces?
A. compaction   B. deposition
C. erosion   D. weathering

11. Metamorphic rock forms as a result of changes in .... and

....in Earth's interior.

12. SEP Evaluate Evidence An igneous rock contains large crystals of quartz, feldspar, and hornblende. How did the rock most likely form?

....

....

13. CCC Identify Patterns A rock sample contains tiny pieces of other rocks that are cemented together. Is it an igneous, sedimentary, or metamorphic rock? Explain your answer.

....

....

....

14. SEP Develop Models ✏ Create a model that represents the formation of sedimentary rock.

4 Cycling of Rocks

MS-ESS2-1

15. Which of the following leads most directly to the production of igneous rock?
A. formation of magma
B. cementation of rocks
C. weathering of rocks
D. deposition of sediment

Use the model of the rock cycle to answer questions 16 and 17.

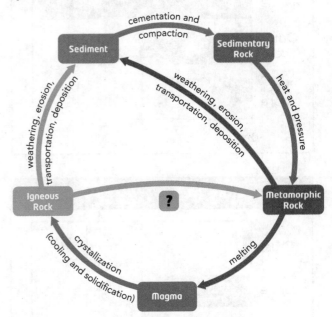

16. Which is the **best** way to complete this model of the rock cycle?
A. crystallization
B. solidification
C. heat and pressure
D. melting

17. What is a step in the process of a rock changing from sedimentary to igneous?
A. crystallization
B. deposition
C. erosion
D. melting

MS-ESS2-1

Evidence-Based Assessment

Earth's layers vary in thickness, temperature, pressure, density, state of matter, and composition. The infographic below compares some of these characteristics of Earth's layers.

Analyze the infographic to answer the questions.

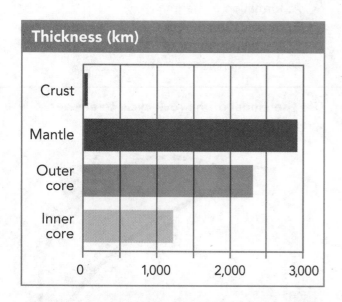

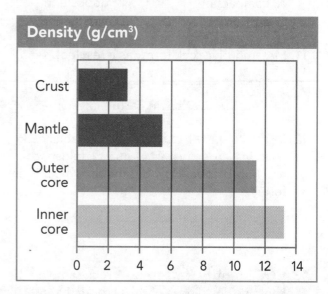

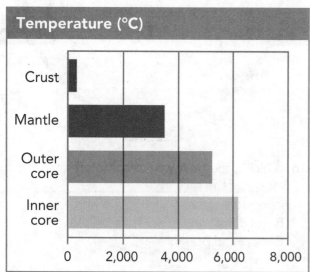

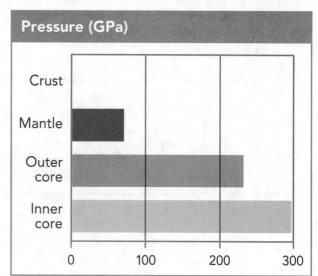

1. **SEP Analyze Data** Which of the following correctly lists Earth's layers from thickest to thinnest?
   A. crust, mantle, outer core, inner core
   B. mantle, outer core, inner core, crust
   C. inner core, outer core, mantle, crust
   D. mantle, crust, outer core, inner core

2. **SEP Analyze Data** About how many times denser is the liquid outer core than the solid crust?
   A. 6   B. 4
   C. 2   D. 3

3. **CCC Cause and Effect** Suppose the mantle were thicker than it is. What effect would this have on the pressure in the outer core? Explain.

   ....
   ....
   ....
   ....
   ....

4. **CCC Patterns** What is the relationship among density, pressure, and temperature across the different layers of Earth? What explains this relationship?

   ....
   ....
   ....
   ....
   ....
   ....
   ....
   ....
   ....
   ....
   ....

5. **Synthesize Information** Both the inner and outer core are made of iron and nickel. The inner core is hotter and denser than the outer core, yet the outer core is in a liquid state and the inner core is solid. Why is this the case? Use evidence from the data tables to support your response.

   ....
   ....
   ....
   ....
   ....
   ....
   ....

Quest FINDINGS

Complete the Quest!

Phenomenon Review and revise the movie scripts. Consider how you can stage readings of the scripts.

Defend Your Claim Do you think producers of fictional films that depict scientific processes should be required to hire a science consultant? Support your opinion with facts and details.

   ....
   ....
   ....
   ....
   ....
   ....

👆 **INTERACTIVITY**

Reflect on Science in the Movies

MS-ESS2-1

The Rock Cycle in Action

Can you make **models** that show **third-grade students** how sedimentary, igneous, and metamorphic **rocks** form?

Background

Phenomenon At first glance, rock formations—such as the Vasquez Rocks in California shown here—don't seem to do much other than sit motionless. But rocks are constantly being cycled through processes that can take just a few minutes or thousands of years.

Your task is to work with a partner to design and build models that could be used to show how the rock cycle works to someone who has never heard of it. Your teacher will assign you a specific type of rock—sedimentary, metamorphic, or igneous—and you will design a model of its formation.

Materials

(per group)

- crayons or crayon rocks of a few different colors
- plastic knife
- paper plates
- aluminum foil
- books or other heavy objects
- hot water or hot plate
- tongs or oven mitts
- beaker

Safety

Be sure to follow all safety guidelines provided by your teacher. Appendix B of your textbook provides more details about the safety icons.

Plan Your Investigation

☐ You will create a plan and design a procedure to model the processes that form the type of rock that has been assigned to you. You must consider:

- the roles that weathering and erosion, deposition, and cementation play in forming sedimentary rock
- the role that high amounts of pressure and energy play in forming metamorphic rock
- the role that high amounts of heat and energy play in forming igneous rock

HANDS-ON LAB

☐ As you design your model, consider these questions:

- What will the different crayons represent in your model?
- How can you use the available materials to represent specific processes such as weathering and erosion, or melting and cementation?
- How can you use the available materials to simulate the processes and flow of energy, such as heat and pressure, that result in the formation of sedimentary, metamorphic, and igneous rocks?

☐ Organize your ideas in the table. Then plan your procedure.

и Demonstrate Go online for a downloadable worksheet for this lab.

Processes	Materials	Notes
1. Weathering and erosion to form sediment		
2. Formation of sedimentary rock		
3. Formation of metamorphic rock		
4. Formation of igneous rock		

Procedure

Use the space below to describe your model(s) and list steps in a procedure to demonstrate the formation of your assigned rock type. You may wish to use sketches to show some steps.

Analyze and Interpret Data

1. **SEP Develop Models** Work with other pairs to develop a complete model of the rock cycle. Draw your model in the space provided. Include labels to explain what each part of the model represents.

2. **Relate Change** Describe the flow of energy and cycling of matter represented by your pair's model. How does your model help you to understand processes that can last thousands of years?

....

....

....

....

3. **Identify Limitations** How does your model differ from the actual rock cycle on Earth? How could you make your model more accurate?

....

....

....

....

....

....

TOPIC

3

Plate Tectonics

NGSS PERFORMANCE EXPECTATIONS

MS-ESS2-2 Construct an explanation based on evidence for how geoscience processes have changed Earth's surface at varying time and spatial scales.

MS-ESS2-3 Analyze and interpret data on the distribution of fossils and rocks, continental shapes, and seafloor structures to provide evidence of the past plate motions.

MS-ESS3-2 Analyze and interpret data on natural hazards to forecast future catastrophic events and inform the development of technologies to mitigate their effects.

How did this island get here?

HANDS-ON LAB

uConnect Explore how Earth's continents can be linked together.

GO ONLINE
to access your
digital course

 VIDEO

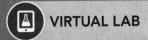 INTERACTIVITY

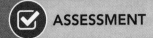 VIRTUAL LAB

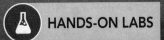 ASSESSMENT

 eTEXT

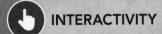 HANDS-ON LABS

The Essential Question

How do geological processes change Earth's surface?

CCC Cause and Effect This island in the South Pacific formed as the result of a violent eruption of material from deep inside Earth. What role does this kind of event play in shaping Earth's surface?

....

....

....

....

....

....

Quest KICKOFF

How safe is it to hike around Mount Rainier?

STEM > **Phenomenon** Camping and hiking in the mountains are popular pastimes for people all over the world. But what if the mountain is actually an active volcano? It hasn't erupted for thousands of years—but it *could*. Would volcanologists say it is safe to hike? What kinds of data do they collect to predict eruptions? In this problem-based Quest activity, you will determine whether it is safe to take an extended camping and hiking trip on Mount Rainier. Through hands-on labs and digital activities, you'll gather evidence about Rainier's history and look into current research on the mountain's volcanic activity. You will use this information to create a presentation that supports your claim and synthesizes your findings.

NBC LEARN ▶ VIDEO

After watching the Quest Kickoff video, which explains volcanic processes, think about the pros and cons of hiking on Mount Rainier. Record your ideas.

PROS

....

....

....

CONS

....

....

....

👆 **INTERACTIVITY**

To Hike or Not to Hike

MS-ESS2-2 Construct an explanation based on evidence for how geoscience processes have changed Earth's surface at varying time and spatial scales.

MS-ESS3-2 Analyze and interpret data on natural hazards to forecast future catastrophic events and inform the development of technologies to mitigate their effects.

Quest CHECK-IN

IN LESSON 1

STEM What is Mount Rainier's history of eruption? Investigate the mountain range's history and draw conclusions about the likelihood of an eruption.

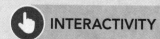

HANDS-ON LAB

Patterns in the Cascade Range

Quest CHECK-IN

IN LESSON 2

How is volcanic activity related to tectonic plate movements? Explore the science behind the connection.

👆 **INTERACTIVITY**

Mount Rainier's Threat

Quest CHECK-IN

IN LESSON 3

What processes cause earthquakes and tsunamis to form? Think about the possible risks caused by movements of the ground beneath your feet.

👆 **INTERACTIVITY**

Monitoring a Volcano

The Cascade Range stretches from northern California all the way up through British Columbia, Canada. Mount Rainier is just one of many volcanoes that lie within the range and are considered "active."

Quest CHECK-IN

STEM IN LESSON 4

What kinds of data can be used to predict an eruption? Investigate the tools and methods that volcanologists use to study volcanoes. Then analyze some data to determine the likelihood of an eruption.

HANDS-ON LAB

Signs of Eruption?

Quest FINDINGS

Complete the Quest!

Present information on Mount Rainier's history and current geological research, along with your evidence-based argument about whether it is safe to hike and camp there.

👆 INTERACTIVITY

Reflect on Mount Rainier's Safety

How Are Earth's Continents Linked Together?

How can you **interpret data** to infer evidence of moving continents?

Background

Phenomenon Your science classroom most likely has a globe sitting on a shelf. Have you ever examined it closely? Are there any features that you find interesting? In this activity, you will make observations of a globe and look for evidence of moving continents.

Materials

(per group)

- globe that shows physical features
- colored markers or crayons
- paper (optional)
- scissors (optional)

Develop a Model

1. Search the globe for two of Earth's features that occur frequently. List them.

....

2. ✂ **SEP Develop a Model** Use the materials to help you make a model of Earth. As you develop your model think about features that will help provide evidence. You may want to develop a legend.

3. **SEP Use a Model** Use your model to find evidence of moving continents.

4. Record your observations.

Observations

HANDS-ON LAB

Connect Go online
for a downloadable
worksheet of this lab.

Analyze and Conclude

1. **SEP Use Models** About how much of Earth's surface is covered
   by the Pacific Ocean? Identify at least two major mountain chains
   that extend over more than one continent.

   ....

   ....

   ....

2. **CCC Patterns** Did you notice any patterns in the shape of the
   continents? Give an example.

   ....

   ....

   ....

3. **SEP Cite Evidence** What evidence did you observe that
   indicates that the continents might have moved over time?

   ....

   ....

   ....

97B

Evidence of Plate Motions

Guiding Questions

- What evidence supported the hypothesis of continental drift?
- What roles do mid-ocean ridges and ocean trenches play in the movement of plates?

Connection

Literacy Cite Textual Evidence

MS-ESS2-3

HANDS-ON LAB

uInvestigate Piece Pangaea together.

Vocabulary

mid-ocean ridge
sea-floor
  spreading
subduction
ocean trench

Academic Vocabulary

hypothesis

Connect It!

✎ Draw lines between South America and Africa to show how the contours of the two continents could fit together.

CCC Stability and Change What might you infer about South America and Africa if you thought the continents were movable objects?

....

Hypothesis of Continental Drift

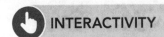
INTERACTIVITY

Try your hand at piecing together puzzles.

For many centuries, scientists and map-makers had been curious about why some continents look as though they could fit together like the pieces of a jigsaw puzzle. The continents on the east and west sides of the South Atlantic Ocean, for example, looked like they would fit together perfectly (**Figure 1**). In the mid 1800s, scientists began to gather clues that suggested the slow movement, or drift, of continents. In 1912, German meteorologist Alfred Wegener (VAY guh nur) further developed the **hypothesis** that all of of the continents had once been fused together, and that over time they had drifted apart. This hypothesis became known as "continental drift."

In 1915, after gathering evidence that supported the hypothesis, Wegener published *The Origin of Continents and Oceans*. The book connected clues from studies of land features, fossils, and climate to make a compelling case for the hypothesis that a supercontinent called Pangaea (pan JEE uh) had broken up into the continents we know today.

Academic Vocabulary

In science, a hypothesis is an idea that can be tested by experimentation or investigation. It is an evidence-based idea that serves as a starting point, whereas a scientific theory is what science produces when a hypothesis has been shown to be true through a broad range of studies. As you read this lesson, highlight or underline the key components of the hypothesis of continental drift.

Pieces of the Puzzle

Figure 1 Scientists wondered whether the continents' coastlines seemed to fit like jigsaw puzzle pieces because they had once been joined together.

Evidence From Land Features There were other pieces of evidence to support the hypothesis of continental drift. Mountain ranges near those continents' coasts seemed to line up, as though they had been made in the same place and at the same time. Coal deposits, made of the remains of plants that thrived in warm locations millions of years ago, were found on multiple continents and in regions that no longer supported that kind of plant life. The separate, scattered locations of these features (**Figure 2**) suggested that they hadn't always been separate.

Evidence From Fossils

Geologists noticed that evidence from the fossil record supported continental drift. (**Figure 2**). Fossils are traces of organisms preserved in rock. Geologist Edward Suess noted that fossils of *Glossopteris* (glaw SAHP tuh ris), a fernlike plant from 250 million years ago, were found on five continents. This suggested that those landmasses had once been connected, as part of Pangaea. Fossils of animals told a similar story. *Mesosaurus* was a reptile that lived in fresh-water habitats millions of years ago, yet *Mesosaurus* fossils were found in both South America and Africa.

Evidence for Continental Drift

Figure 2 Study the map key to see how Wegener pieced together similar pieces of evidence from separate sites to support his hypothesis.

Interpret Visuals Present-day India is in South Asia, at the northern end of the Indian Ocean. What evidence found in India matches that of other locations?

....

....

....

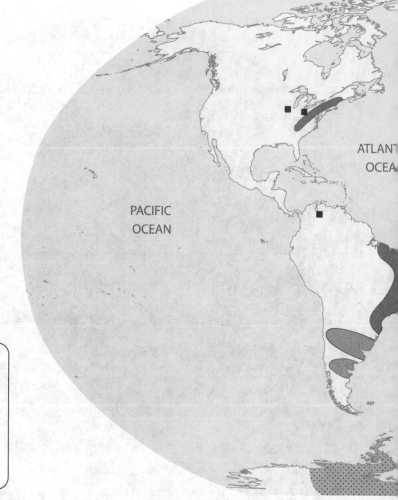

ATLANTIC
OCEAN

PACIFIC
OCEAN

KEY
- Folded mountains
- Coal beds
- Glacial deposits
- *Glossopteris* fossils
- *Lystrosaurus* fossils
- *Mesosaurus* fossils

Evidence From Climate Wegener, whose own expertise was in the study of weather and climate and not geology, also gathered evidence that showed Earth's continents had experienced different climates than the ones they have today. For example, Spitsbergen, an island in the Arctic Ocean, has fossils of plants that could have survived only in a tropical climate. This doesn't mean that the Arctic Ocean once had a tropical climate. That isn't possible, because the poles do not receive enough sunlight to produce tropical weather or support tropical plants. Instead, this evidence means Spitsbergen used to be at the equator, part of a supercontinent. The supercontinent slowly broke apart, and the island now known as Spitsbergen drifted far to the north over the course of millions of years.

✓ READING CHECK **Summarize Text** What is the general pattern in the evidence that supports the hypothesis of continental drift?

....

....

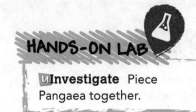

HANDS-ON LAB

✎**Investigate** Piece Pangaea together.

▤**Reflect** Think of some organic item (such as a flower or type of fruit) that you've found in at least two places that are many miles apart. Do the items have a common origin? Why do you think so? What conclusions can you draw from the item's presence in widely-different locations?

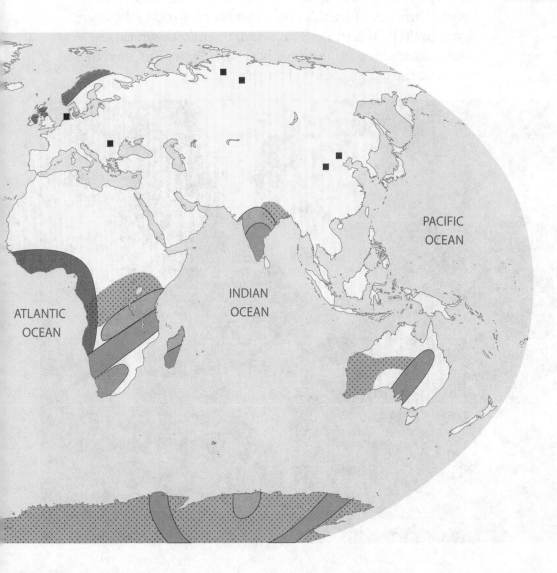

PACIFIC OCEAN

ATLANTIC OCEAN

INDIAN OCEAN

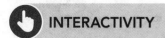

INTERACTIVITY

Investigate patterns on land and on the seafloor.

Mid-Ocean Ridges

Figure 3 Mapping of mid-ocean ridges in the mid-twentieth century provided supporting evidence that Earth's surface was composed of moving plates.

Interpret Visuals Do any of the mid-ocean ridges appear to extend into continents? Which ones?

....

....

....

Mid-Ocean Ridges

The hypothesis of continental drift included evidence from different areas of science, but it had a major flaw. It lacked a good explanation for *how* the continents could have broken up and moved apart. Many scientists rejected the hypothesis for that reason. By the middle of the twentieth century, advances in oceanography—the study of Earth's oceans—allowed a mapping of the ocean floor that renewed interest in continental drift. Undersea exploration provided evidence that Earth's surface was composed of moving plates—large pieces of the lithosphere.

By measuring distances from the sea surface to its floor, scientists now had a clear visual of what Earth's surface looked like under the oceans. What surprised many was the presence of long, zipper-like chains of undersea mountains called **mid-ocean ridges**. One such chain, called the Mid-Atlantic Ridge, ran down the middle of the Atlantic Ocean, curving in a pattern that seemed to mirror the contours of the surrounding continental coastlines. Further modeling and mapping of the ocean floor in the 1990s showed that these mid-ocean ridges extend throughout Earth's oceans for about 70,000 kilometers. If you could hold Earth in your hand, the mid-ocean ridges might resemble the seams on a baseball (**Figure 3**). Could these ridges be the actual seams of Earth's crust?

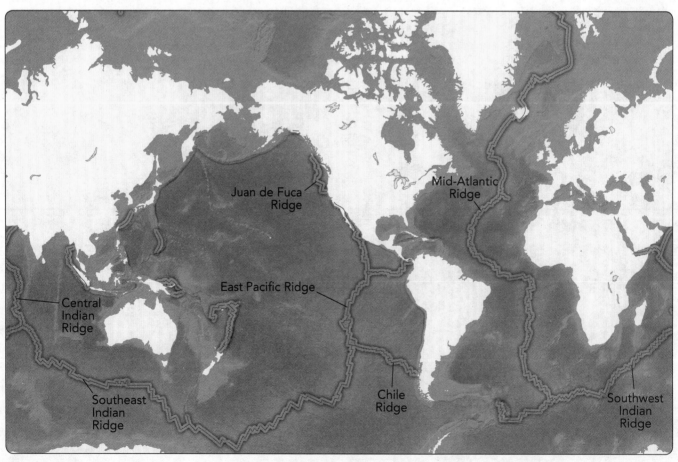

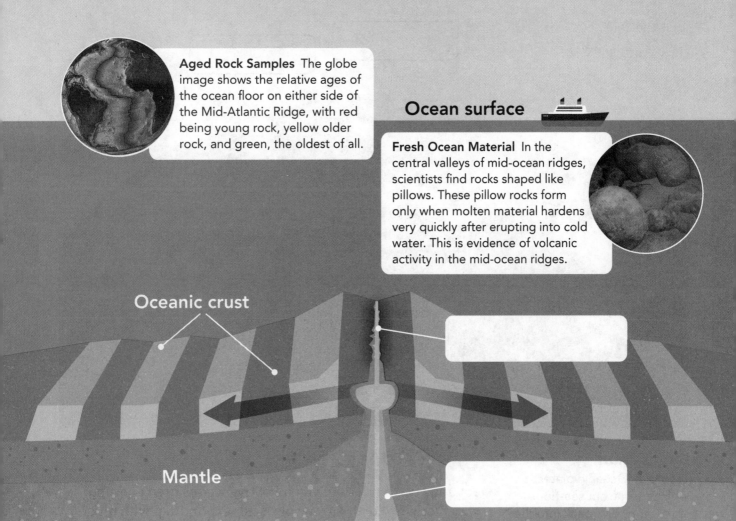

Aged Rock Samples The globe image shows the relative ages of the ocean floor on either side of the Mid-Atlantic Ridge, with red being young rock, yellow older rock, and green, the oldest of all.

Ocean surface

Fresh Ocean Material In the central valleys of mid-ocean ridges, scientists find rocks shaped like pillows. These pillow rocks form only when molten material hardens very quickly after erupting into cold water. This is evidence of volcanic activity in the mid-ocean ridges.

Oceanic crust

Mantle

Sea-Floor Spreading

While ocean-floor mapping was underway, geologists began to gather samples of rock from the ocean floor. They learned that mid-ocean ridges are the sources of new spans of the ocean floor. In a process called **sea-floor spreading**, molten rock flows up through a crack in Earth's crust and hardens into solid strips of new rock on both sides of the crack. The entire floor on either side of the ridge moves away when this occurs, meaning the older strips of rock move farther from the ridge over time. It's like a two-way conveyer belt with new material appearing at the ridge while older material is carried farther away. **Figure 4** shows a model and describes some specific evidence of sea-floor spreading.

READING CHECK **Cite Textual Evidence** Why was undersea exploration important for developing the theory of plate tectonics?

Sea-Floor Spreading
Figure 4 Sea-floor spreading continually adds material to the ocean floor on both sides of the ridge.

SEP Develop Models 🖊 Label the different features that play a role in sea-floor spreading.

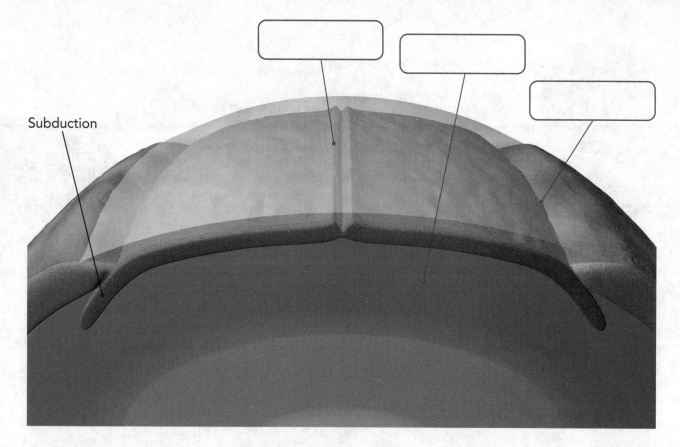

Subduction

Subduction

Figure 5 Oceanic plates, which form from sea-floor spreading, sink back into the mantle at subduction zones.

CCC System Models
Label the mantle, mid-ocean ridge, and ocean trench.

▶ **VIDEO**

Watch what happens at ocean ridges and trenches.

Ocean Trenches

You may be wondering why all of the oceans aren't getting wider, or why Earth as a whole is not expanding, with all of the sea-floor spreading going on. The answer to that is **subduction** (sub DUC shun), or the sinking movement of ocean floor back into the mantle. Subduction occurs where a dense plate of oceanic crust goes under an adjacent section of Earth's crust. This occurs at **ocean trenches**, which are undersea valleys that are the deepest parts of the ocean (**Figure 5**).

The Process of Subduction New oceanic crust is relatively warm. As the rock cools and moves away from a mid-ocean ridge, it gets denser. At some point, the dense slab of oceanic crust may meet another section of ocean floor, or a continent. What happens? Because the oceanic crust is cooler than the mantle underneath, it is denser and will sink into the mantle if given the chance. At an ocean trench, it has that chance, and the oceanic crust will sink under the edge of a continent or a younger, less-dense slab of oceanic crust. The oceanic plate that sinks back into the mantle gets recycled. This process can produce volcanic eruptions at the surface. If the oceanic crust meets continental crust, then a chain of volcanoes will form. If it meets more oceanic crust, then there will likely be a chain of volcanic islands.

Subduction and the Oceans An ocean basin can have a spreading ridge, subduction zones, or both, depending on its age. An ocean basin starts with just a spreading ridge. The Atlantic Ocean, for example, has the Mid-Atlantic Ridge running down its full length, but no subduction zones. This means that the Atlantic Ocean is still getting wider—by about 2 to 5 centimeters per year. At some point, part of the oceanic plate will begin to sink back into the mantle and a subduction zone will form.

The Pacific Ocean is a more mature ocean basin. While it still has a spreading ridge, the Pacific basin is surrounded by subduction zones. The oceanic crust in the Pacific is being recycled back into the mantle faster than it is being created. This means that the Pacific Ocean basin is getting smaller.

Eventually, hundreds of millions of years from now, as Africa collides into Europe and the Pacific Ocean closes up, a new supercontinent may appear.

✓ READING CHECK **Cite Textual Evidence** What features are evidence of the Pacific Ocean's maturity?

👆 **INTERACTIVITY**

Learn about the slow and steady movement on Earth.

Model It

Predict North America's Movement
Figure 6 The map shows the layout of some of Earth's landmasses, the mid-ocean ridges where plates are made, and ocean trenches where plates are recycled.

CCC Stability and Change 🖊 Draw a line to indicate where you think the west coast of North America will eventually be located.

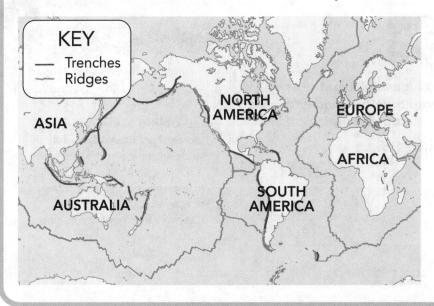

KEY
— Trenches
— Ridges

ASIA

NORTH AMERICA

EUROPE

AFRICA

SOUTH AMERICA

AUSTRALIA

☑LESSON 1 Check

MS-ESS2-3

1. **SEP Communicate Information** Describe the hypothesis of continental drift.

....

....

....

....

2. **SEP Analyze Data** How did the study of fossils provide support for the ideas behind the existence of Pangaea?

....

....

....

....

....

....

....

....

3. **SEP Interpret Data** How did the discovery of mid-ocean ridges support the hypothesis of continental drift?

....

....

....

4. **CCC Cause and Effect** A large oceanic crust collides with the edge of a continent. What will happen?

....

....

....

5. **Infer** A remotely-operated vehicle is sent to the deepest part of the Mariana Trench. It returns with a sample of rock from the ocean floor. Would this rock be old or young? Explain.

....

....

....

....

....

....

....

....

Quest CHECK-IN

In this lesson you learned about Wegener's hypothesis of continental drift and how he pieced together evidence from different areas of natural history to support his hypothesis.

Connect to the Nature of Science How can the history of Mount Rainier's eruptions help you decide whether hiking around Mount Rainier is safe?

....

....

....

HANDS-ON LAB

Patterns in the Cascade Range

Go online to download the lab worksheet. Analyze data to determine whether there is a pattern to Mount Rainier's eruptions and those of other nearby volcanoes in the Cascade Range of the Pacific Northwest.

MS-ESS2-3

The Slow Acceptance of
Continental Drift

"Utter rot," a "fairy tale," and "delirious ravings." These statements are how some scientists in the early 1900s responded to Alfred Wegener's book describing the hypothesis continental drift.

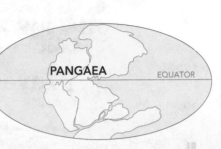

PANGAEA   EQUATOR

CONNECT TO YOU

Do you think skepticism is an important quality for a scientist to have? Why or why not? Discuss your ideas with a partner.

This case demonstrates that scientific thought doesn't always advance neatly or without controversy. Long-held scientific attitudes can be slow to change when new evidence or interpretations are encountered.

The hypothesis of continental drift faced a number of challenges. Though there was evidence to support it, there was not a convincing explanation of how continental drift actually occurred. Scientists who were already skeptical of the idea only heaped additional ridicule on Wegener.

In addition, Wegener was a trained meteorologist, but the hypothesis crossed multiple scientific disciplines. Many experts in their respective fields felt threatened because Wegener—viewed as an outsider—challenged their authority and expertise. After his death in 1930, continental drift was virtually ignored.

Over the next few decades, advances in technology led to a better understanding of the geological forces that shape Earth's surface. By the early 1960s, younger geologists were able to explain the mechanism by which the continents moved. The ideas behind continental drift re-emerged as the theory of plate tectonics.

Wegener often took research trips to Greenland to study its climate. By taking core samples of ice, climatologists can learn about the climate of the past.

Plate Tectonics and Earth's Surface

Guiding Questions

- How do Earth's plates move?
- How do Earth's surface features support the theory of plate tectonics?
- What are the products of plate movement at different scales?

Connections

Literacy Integrate With Visuals

Math Reason Quantitatively

MS-ESS2-2

HANDS-ON LAB

uInvestigate Explore different plate interactions.

Vocabulary

divergent boundary
convergent boundary
transform boundary

Academic Vocabulary

theory

Connect It!

✏️ **Identify where the Himalayan Mountains are and circle them.**

CCC Stability and Change Scientists are measuring Mount Everest to determine whether its height has changed. Why would the Himalayas be getting taller?

....

....

....

The Theory of Plate Tectonics

With observations of many geologists in the 1950s and 1960s, particularly of the features of the ocean floor, the ideas behind continental drift re-emerged as the **theory** of plate tectonics. This theory states that Earth's lithosphere—the crust and upper part of the mantle—is broken up into distinct plates. The plates are puzzle-like pieces that are in slow, constant motion relative to each other due to forces within the mantle. The theory explains the specific patterns of motion among the plates, including the different types of boundaries where they meet and the events and features that occur at their boundaries (**Figure 1**). The term *tectonic* refers to Earth's crust and to the large-scale processes that occur within it.

HANDS-ON LAB

Investigate the role of stress in changing Earth's surface.

Academic Vocabulary

In science, the term *theory* is applied only to ideas that are supported by a vast, diverse array of evidence. How is the term used in everyday life?

....

....

....

....

....

....

Plate Tectonics Give Rise to the Himalayas

Figure 1 The tallest mountains on Earth, K2 and Mount Everest, are part of the Himalayas. When the landmass that is now known as India collided with Asia, these mountains began to form.

Convection Currents

Figure 2 In a pot of boiling water, warmer water rises and cooler water sinks to fill the void. This movement creates convection currents in the pot of water.

Convection Drives Plate Motions

The tectonic plates move because they are part of convection currents in the mantle. You may recall that convection is a cyclical movement of fluid driven by temperature differences at the top and bottom, such as cold water sinking from the surface and warm water rising from below (**Figure 2**). Convection occurs in the mantle where solid rock flows in slow-moving currents. These currents are responsible for moving the continents great distances across Earth's surface, even if they move at speeds too slow to be noticed.

Types of Crust

Plates consist of one or two types of crust. Oceanic crust is the dense type of crust that is found at the bottom of the ocean (**Figure 3**). Some plates, such as the Pacific Plate, consist entirely of oceanic crust. The other type of crust is called continental crust. It is less dense than oceanic crust and is almost always thicker. As a result, the surfaces of continents are above sea level.

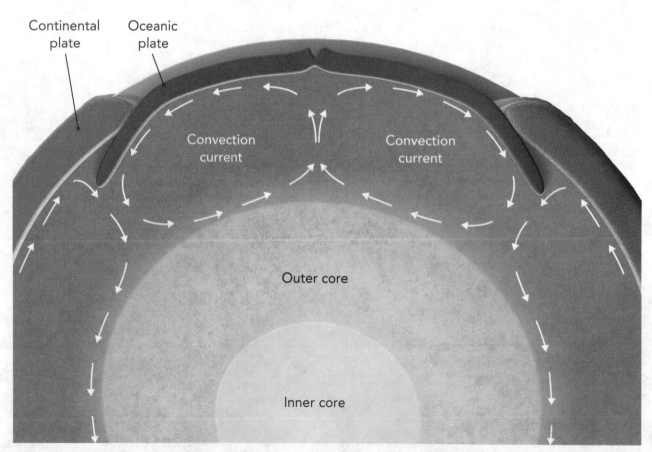

Oceanic and Continental Crust

Figure 3 The very dense crust of the ocean floor is oceanic crust. Crust that is less dense can be thick enough that it's above sea level. Continental crust gets its name from the fact that the surfaces of continents are mostly above sea level.

Interpret Visuals Use the directions in which the convection currents are moving in the figure to draw in arrows indicating the direction of the oceanic plates.

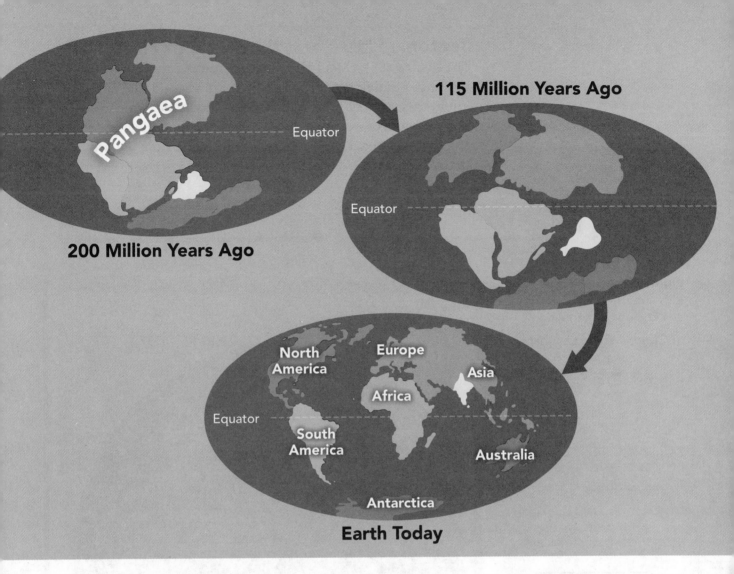

Pangaea

200 Million Years Ago

115 Million Years Ago

Equator

Equator

North America

Europe

Asia

Africa

Equator

South America

Australia

Antarctica

Earth Today

Plate Motions Over Time Scientists use satellites to measure plate motions precisely. The plates move very slowly—about 1 to 10 centimeters per year. The North American and Eurasian plates, named for the continents they carry, move apart at a rate of 1 to 2 centimeters per year, or about as fast as your fingernails grow. Because the plates have been moving for billions of years, they have moved great distances.

Over time, the movement of Earth's plates has greatly changed the locations of the continents and the size and shape of the ocean basins. Long before Pangaea existed, over billions of years, other supercontinents had formed and split apart. Pangaea itself formed when Earth's landmasses moved together about 350 to 250 million years ago. Then, about 200 million years ago, Pangaea began to break apart (**Figure 4**).

☑ READING CHECK **Draw Conclusions** When might the continents we know today form a new supercontinent?

....

200 Million Years of Plate Motions

Figure 4 It has taken the continents about 200 million years to move to their present locations, since the breakup of Pangaea.

Interpret Visuals ✏
Label the landmasses from 115 million years ago with the present-day names of landmasses, as shown on the "Earth Today" map.

 **INTERACTIVITY**

Compare the relative rates of motion of different plates.

Tectonic Plates and the "Ring of Fire"

The theory of plate tectonics predicts that earthquakes and volcanoes should occur at plate boundaries, and that some landforms, such as mountain ranges, should mark the plate boundaries. For example, many volcanic eruptions and earthquakes occur at the edges of the Pacific Plate (**Figure 5**), that lies under the Pacific Ocean.

Model It!

Ring of Fire

Figure 5 Because the region around the Pacific Ocean is prone to volcanic activity and earthquakes, it is known as the "Ring of Fire."

1. **Claim** Why do so many volcanoes seem to occur on coastlines of the Pacific Ocean?

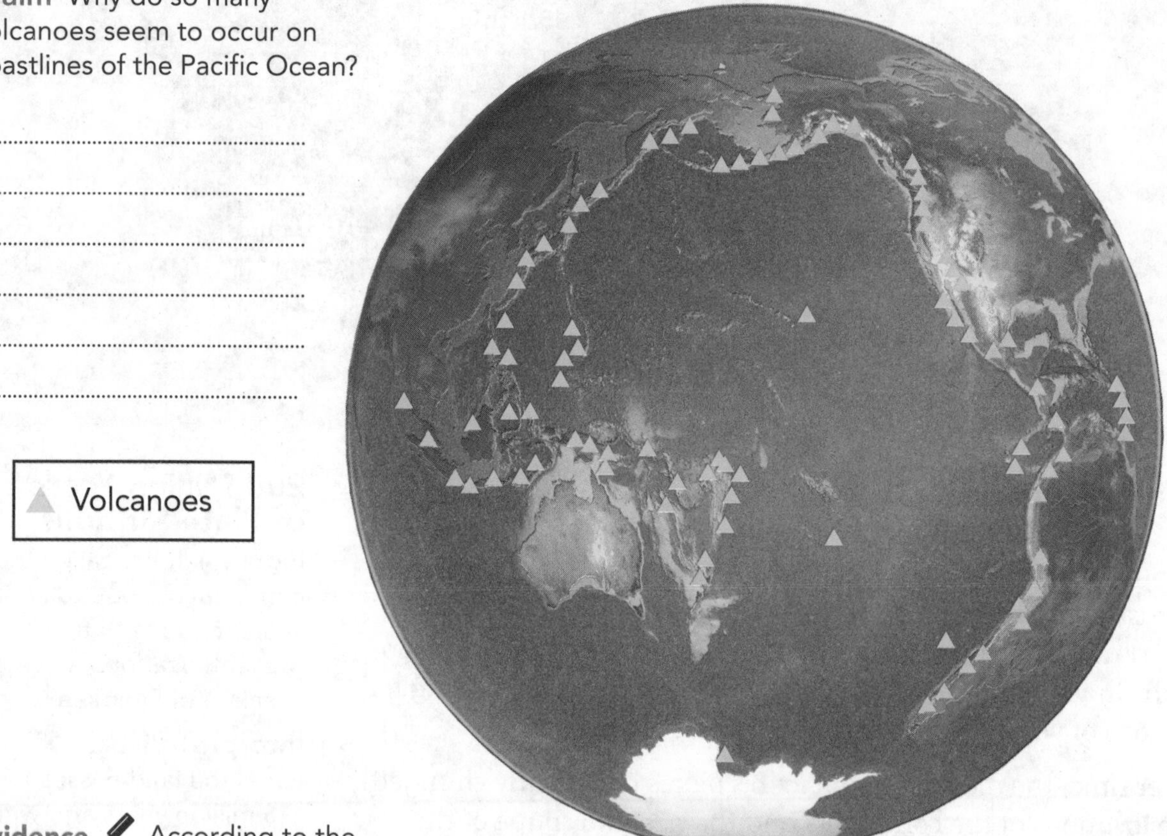

....
....
....
....
....
....

▲ Volcanoes

2. **Evidence** 🖊 According to the theory of plate tectonics, how do the locations of volcanoes compare with plate boundaries? On **Figure 5**, draw the edges of the different plates, including the Pacific Plate. Use **Figure 6** to help you.

3. **Reasoning** Describe how the symbols on the map guided your mark-up of the map.

....
....

Plate Map

Figure 6 🖊 Earth scientists have identified the different tectonic plates, many of which are named for the continents they carry. The boundaries have been identified as convergent, divergent, or transform. Relative plate movements at some of the boundaries are indicated with red arrows.

SEP Develop Models 🖊 Using the map key as a reference, add the arrows that are missing in the circles provided.

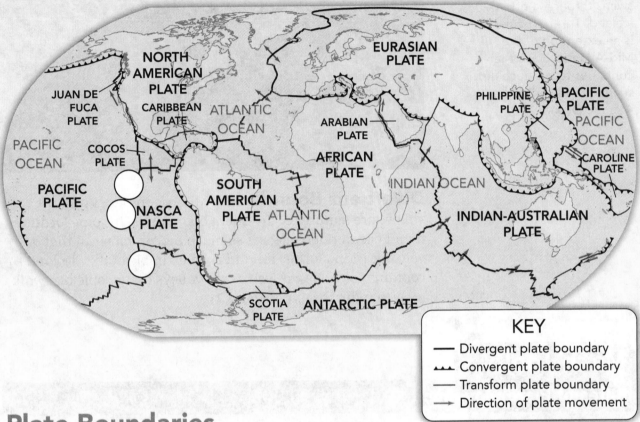

KEY

— Divergent plate boundary
⩜⩜ Convergent plate boundary
— Transform plate boundary
→ Direction of plate movement

Plate Boundaries

Earth's plates meet and interact at boundaries. Along each boundary, plates move in one of three ways. Plates move apart, or diverge, from each other at a **divergent boundary** (dy VUR junt). Plates come together, or converge, at a **convergent boundary** (kun VER junt). Plates slip past each other along a **transform boundary**. The interactions of plates at boundaries produce great changes on land and on the ocean floor. These changes include the formation of volcanoes, mountain ranges, and deep-ocean trenches. Earthquakes and the triggering of tsunamis are also more common at or near plate boundaries. **Figure 6** depicts the major tectonic plates and the types of boundaries between them.

✓ READING CHECK **Integrate With Visuals** Which of the plates from the map would be a good starting point for a diagram that summarizes the different boundaries? Why?

....

....

Literacy Connection

Integrate With Visuals
In your science notebook, draw sketches of the different interactions at plate boundaries. Work toward a visual presentation that summarizes the plate boundaries in a single diagram.

👆 **INTERACTIVITY**

Explore surface features associated with plate movement at different locations around the world.

113

▶ VIDEO

Learn about the tectonic plate boundary types.

Iceland

Figure 7 A scuba diver swims through a rift in Iceland. This particular rift is an extension of the Mid-Atlantic Ridge that continues to produce new seafloor and widen the Atlantic Ocean.

Divergent Boundaries Mid-ocean ridges and rift valleys are features of divergent boundaries. In some locations, a mid-ocean ridge releases so much molten material that a volcanic island forms. Iceland is an example of this. Iceland contains volcanoes as well as rift valleys that people can walk or even swim through (**Figure 7**).

Math Toolbox

Rates of Plate Movement

Earth scientists measure plate movement by using the Global Positioning System (GPS) of satellites. Receivers anchored in Earth's surface receive signals from satellites, and calculate their positions using the time it takes for signals to be received. Over time, changes in those signal times indicate plate movement.

1. **Reason Quantitatively** Evidence from GPS readings suggests that the Mid-Atlantic Ridge spreads about 2.5 cm per year. How fast is the North American Plate moving away from the ridge? Explain your answer.

....

....

....

....

....

2. **SEP Use Mathematics** The Pacific Plate moves to the northwest at an average rate of 10 cm per year. Hawaii is in the middle of the Pacific Plate, 6,600 kilometers southeast of Japan, which is on the edge of several adjacent plates. If the Pacific Plate continues to move at the same rate and in the same direction, when will Hawaii collide with Japan? Show your work.

....

....

....

....

Convergent Boundaries

Convergent Boundaries A boundary where two plates collide, or move toward each other, is called a convergent boundary. If two continents collide, then a mountain range is pushed up. This is how the Himalayas formed, and are still being pushed up. What is now India used to be a separate continent that broke away from Antarctica and headed north. It began colliding with Asia more than 60 million years ago, and the edges of the two plates folded like the hoods of two cars in a head-on collision (**Figure 8**). Mount Everest and the rest of the Himalayas are the result.

If one or both plates are oceanic, then subduction occurs. The ocean plate always subducts if it collides with a continent. If two oceanic plates collide, the older, colder, and denser plate usually subducts beneath the younger plate, with an ocean trench marking the plate boundary. As the subducting plate sinks back into the mantle, water that was in the ocean crust rises into the overlying mantle, lowering its melting point. Magma forms and rises up through the overlying plate, producing volcanoes. On land, this results in the formation of volcanic mountains. Mountains can also form as ocean seafloor sediments are scraped onto the edge of the overlying plate, forming a large wedge of rock.

Under the sea, subduction produces undersea volcanoes, also known as seamounts. If they grow tall enough, these volcanoes form a volcanic island chain. This is why there are often chains of volcanic islands where convergent boundaries exist in the ocean.

HANDS-ON LAB

ᴜ**Investigate** Explore different plate interactions.

Collision at a Convergent Boundary

Figure 8 When two continental plates collide, their collision can have a crumpling effect on the crust that produces tall mountains, just as when two cars crash in a head-on collision. If one plate is denser, such as a plate of oceanic crust, that denser plate will dive under the other. This can also produce mountains as the overlying plate edge is nudged upward.

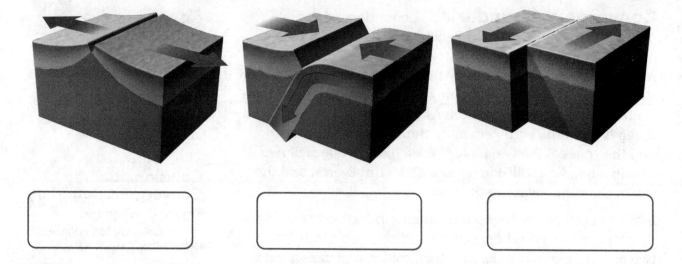

[ ] [ ] [ ]

Types of Plate Boundaries

Figure 9 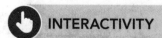 The three types of plate boundaries are modeled here. Label each illustration with the term that describes the boundary.

INTERACTIVITY

Investigate how stress is built up and released at faults.

Transform Boundaries Plates slide past each other at a transform boundary. Earthquakes occur here on faults called transform faults. Bending across a fault occurs when the two sides remain locked together. When enough stress builds up, the fault ruptures and an earthquake occurs. This is what causes earthquakes along transform faults such as the San Andreas Fault in California. In some cases a surface feature (such as a stream or road) that crossed a fault is visibly offset after a major slippage of the plates. Depending on how the plate edges match up, a vertical offset can exist across the fault.

Keep in mind that the tectonic plates of Earth's lithosphere are three-dimensional objects that are moving around a sphere. The shapes of the plates are irregular. This means every plate has some mixture of the different types of boundaries, and at some point the boundaries may change as the plates shrink, grow, collide, slip past each other, subduct, and so on. Interactions among tectonic plates continue to reshape Earth's surface features.

[✓] READING CHECK **Summarize Text** What happens at divergent, convergent, and transform boundaries?

....

....

....

1. Compare and Contrast At what type of plate boundary would you find a rift valley that is growing wider?

....

2. SEP Interpret Data Describe what is going on in this diagram.

....

....

....

....

....

3. CCC Cause and Effect What other surface feature that is not shown in the diagram could be produced as a result of the process shown?

....

4. SEP Use Mathematics It takes 100,000 years for a plate to move about 2 kilometers. What is that plate's rate of motion in centimeters per year?

....

5. Connect to Nature of Science What does the theory of plate tectonics have that Wegener's hypothesis of continental drift did not have?

....

....

....

....

....

....

Quest CHECK-IN

In this lesson, you learned about the specific mechanisms by which plates move and how interactions of tectonic plates affect Earth's surface.

SEP Construct Explanations What's the connection between Mount Rainier and the plate boundaries along the coast of the Pacific Northwest?

....

....

....

INTERACTIVITY

Mount Rainier's Threat

Go online to learn how Mount Rainier and other volcanic mountains in the Cascade Range formed as a result of geologic activity at tectonic plate boundaries.

117

AUSTRALIA
on the Move

Located on one of the world's fastest moving tectonic plates—the Australian Plate—Australia is moving about 7 centimeters north, and slightly east, each year.

A Kangaroo's Length

The movement of Australia requires updates to its official location on maps. In 2017, it moved 1.5 meters north. This is about the length of a gray kangaroo.

Australia's plate, of course, is not the only moving plate on Earth. But each of the planet's plates moves at a different rate. Most move at a rate of a few centimeters a year. At 7 centimeters a year, Australia is one of the fastest.

In the 1960s, geologists confirmed that tectonic plates move along Earth's mantle. But only recently, with the help of computer modeling, have they come to understand why the plates move at different speeds. As a plate sinks into the mantle at a subduction zone, it pulls along the rest of the plate. It's similar to what happens to all the dishes and glasses on a dinner table when you pull the tablecloth down on one side. The size and structure of the subduction zone influence the strength of this pull. A large plate edge that is descending into the mantle at a large subduction zone would exert more force on the rest of the plate.

Measuring Movement

No one can feel the plates moving. They move only about as fast as your fingernails grow. But the movement adds up. In 50 million years, the Australian Plate could collide with Southeast Asia.

Over time, the continent's movement means that Australia's latitude and longitude on older maps no longer match the actual location of the continent. Maps require corrections to compensate for Australia's movement.

Australia has officially changed its location four times in the last 50 years. At the beginning of 2017, Australia changed its location once again, this time moving it another 1.5 meters (about 5 feet) north.

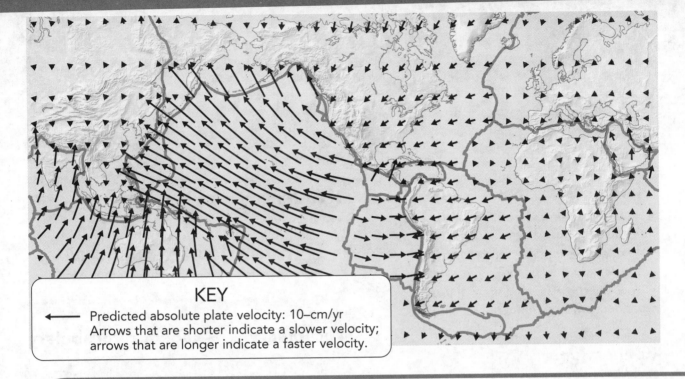

KEY

← Predicted absolute plate velocity: 10–cm/yr
Arrows that are shorter indicate a slower velocity;
arrows that are longer indicate a faster velocity.

**Use this map and Figure 6 in Lesson 2 to answer the
following questions.**

1. **Summarize** What factors affect the speed at which a tectonic
   plate moves?

   ....

   ....

2. **Interpret Data** Which plate is moving fastest? Cite evidence to
   justify your answer.

   ....

   ....

3. **Apply Concepts** Would you expect a largely oceanic plate to
   move faster than a largely continental plate? Explain.

   ....

   ....

   ....

   ....

4. **Construct Explanations** The Australian and Pacific plates are
   among the fastest-moving plates. What conclusions can you draw
   about the subduction zone where the Australian Plate meets the
   Pacific Plate? Use evidence from the text and the map to support
   your explanation.

   ....

   ....

119

LESSON 3

Earthquakes and Tsunami Hazards

Guiding Questions

- How do plate movement and stress produce new landforms?
- What are earthquakes and tsunamis, and why do they occur?
- How can the effects of earthquakes and tsunamis be mitigated?

Connections

Literacy Evaluate Media

Math Analyze Graphs

MS-ESS2-2, MS-ESS3-2

HANDS-ON LAB

uInvestigate Analyze data and interpret patterns to predict future earthquakes.

Vocabulary

stress
tension
compression
shearing
fault
earthquake
magnitude
tsunami

Academic Vocabulary

scale

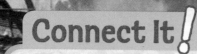

Connect It!

✏️ **Circle and label evidence that a tsunami occurred.**

CCC Cause and Effect How did the ship come to rest on land?

....

....

....

120 Plate Tectonics

Stress and Earth's Crust

The movement of Earth's massive tectonic plates generates tremendous force. This force can bend and break the rock of Earth's crust. The force that acts on rock to change its shape or volume is called **stress**. There are three kinds of stress. **Tension** pulls on Earth's crust, stretching the rock to make it thinner, especially at the point halfway between the two pulling forces. **Compression** squeezes rock until it bends or breaks. When compression occurs at a large scale, rock can be folded into mountains. **Shearing** occurs when rock is being pushed in two opposite directions, to the point that it bends or breaks. These types of stress can produce both folds and faults. Movement of Earth's crust around faults can produce destructive earthquakes and, in some cases, tsunamis (**Figure 1**).

Make Meaning As you go through the lesson, keep notes in your science notebook about how the physical stresses described here are involved in processes that produce earthquakes and tsunamis.

Tsunami Damage
Figure 1 In 2011, a major tsunami engulfed parts of Japan, killing thousands and destroying property.

Normal Fault

A **fault** is a break in the rock of Earth's crust or mantle. Most faults occur along plate boundaries, where stress of one or more types is deforming the rock, leading to changes at Earth's surface (**Figure 2**). The two sides of a fault are referred to as walls. The wall whose rock is over the other is called the hanging wall, and the other is called the footwall. In a normal fault, the hanging wall slips down relative to the footwall (**Figure 3A**). This usually occurs at a divergent plate boundary, where tension is pulling the plates away from each other. If there is a series of normal faults, a slab of crust that falls away can become a valley while the adjacent slabs can become mountains.

Reverse Fault

Compression can produce a reverse fault, in which the hanging wall slides up and over the footwall (**Figure 3B**). The northern Rocky Mountains were gradually lifted by the action at several reverse faults. Reverse faults are common at convergent boundaries.

Strike-Slip Fault

California's San Andreas Fault is a product of shearing. Walls of rock grind past each other in opposite directions, making a strike-slip fault (**Figure 3C**). Transform boundaries are home to strike-slip faults.

☑ READING CHECK **Determine Central Ideas** Pair each fault type with the type of stress that produces it.

....

....

Death Valley

Figure 2 Tension can result in peaks around a sunken valley, such as Death Valley in California.

Types of Faults

Figure 3 ✏ SEP Develop Models The three types of faults are shown here. Complete diagrams A and B by labeling the hanging walls and footwalls. In Diagram C, draw arrows to indicate the direction of shearing force and the movement along the fault.

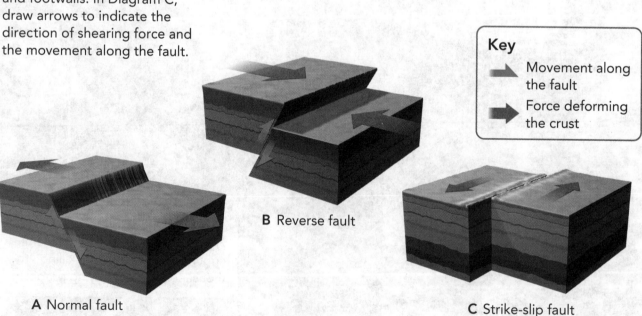

Key

→ Movement along the fault

→ Force deforming the crust

A Normal fault

B Reverse fault

C Strike-slip fault

Valleys and Mountains

Figure 4 As tension pulls rock apart along normal faults, some blocks fall, leaving others elevated. Over time, the resulting mountains weather.

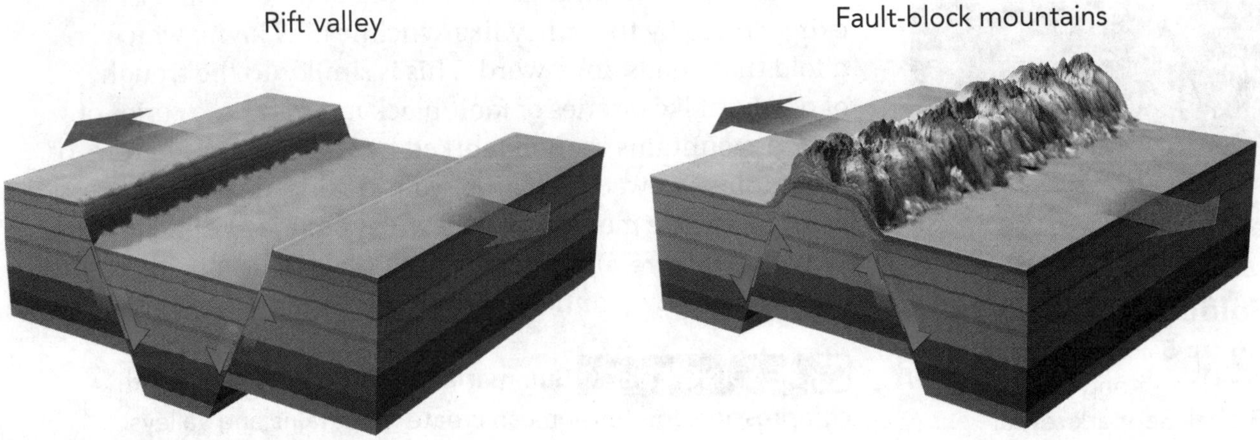

Rift valley

Fault-block mountains

New Landforms From Plate Movement

Over millions of years, the forces of plate movement can change a flat plain into folded mountains, fault-block mountains, and other dramatic features of Earth's surface.

Tension and Normal Faults To see how tension and normal faults produce mountains, we need to zoom out and look at a series of at least two normal faults. Where two plates move away from each other, tension forms numerous faults that run parallel to each other over a wide area. A wedge of rock that has hanging walls at both faults drops down as tension pulls the adjacent footwalls away to form a rift valley (**Figure 4**). This leaves the other blocks higher up, as mountains. Mountains built this way are called fault-block mountains.

Folding Compression within a plate causes the crust to deform without breaking. Folds are bends in rock that form when compression shortens and thickens Earth's crust. Folds may be centimeters across or they may span many kilometers. The folds are often most visible and obvious when the rock is layered. When folding occurs on a large **scale,** folds that bend upward become mountains and folds that bend downward become valleys.

Academic Vocabulary

The processes of plate tectonics occur at different scales of time and space. List some different terms that are used to describe distance and time at vastly different scales.

....

....

....

Folded Mountain

Figure 5 Formations at the Hong Kong UNESCO Global Geopark reveal distinct folding patterns.

Anticlines and Synclines

A fold in rock that bends upward into an arch is called an anticline (AN tih klyn). This may resemble the crest of a wave, as seen in **Figure 5**. Weathering and erosion have shaped many large-scale anticlines into mountains. The height of an anticline is exaggerated by the valley-like syncline (SIN klyn), which is a fold that bends downward. This is similar to the trough of a wave. Like a series of fault-block mountains, a series of folded mountains is often marked by valleys between rows of mountains. Viewed at a large scale, a wide area of compressed crust may have mountains and valleys made of anticlines and synclines (**Figure 6**), while the large-scale folds may themselves contain their own anticlines and synclines.

☑ **READING CHECK** **Summarize Text** Describe how both compression and tension can create mountains and valleys.

....

....

....

....

Anticlines and Synclines as Mountains and Valleys

Figure 6 Label the anticlines and synclines in the diagram.

SEP Evaluate Information 🖊 How does this figure oversimplify how compression produces folds in Earth's crust?

....

....

....

Earthquakes

Some plate interactions are gradual, quiet, and almost imperceptible. Others can be sudden, violent, loud, and destructive. At some faults, the plates may grind to a halt and remain stuck in place for years. Stress builds up until the plates lurch into motion, releasing a great amount of energy. The shaking and trembling that results from this plate movement is an **earthquake**. Some of the energy released in an earthquake is in the form of seismic waves.

Seismic Waves Similar to sound waves, seismic waves are vibrations that travel through Earth carrying energy released by various processes, such as earthquakes, ocean storms, and volcanic eruptions. There are three types of seismic waves, as shown in **Figure 7**. The waves begin at the earthquake's focus, where rock that was under stress begins to break or move. Waves may strike quickest and with the most energy at the point on Earth's surface directly above the earthquake's focus, called the epicenter. But seismic waves also move in all directions, through and across Earth's interior and surface. When seismic waves pass from one material to another, they can change speeds and directions.

HANDS-ON LAB

Investigate Analyze data and interpret patterns to predict future earthquakes.

P and S Waves
Figure 7 SEP Develop Models ✏ The motion of particles in Earth's surface is shown for P waves and S waves. Draw the particle motion for the surface waves.

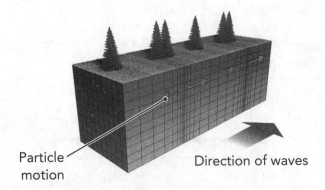

Particle motion — Direction of waves

P waves, short for primary waves, travel the fastest. They are the first to arrive at a location on Earth's surface. P waves compress and expand the ground.

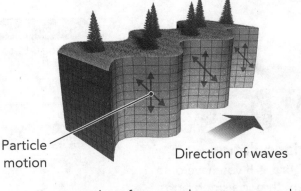

Particle motion — Direction of waves

S waves, short for secondary waves, travel more slowly so they arrive after P waves. S waves can move the ground side to side or up and down, relative to the direction in which they travel..

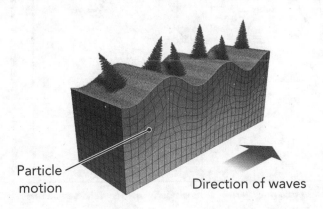

Particle motion — Direction of waves

Surface waves can form when P waves and S waves reach Earth's surface. The result can be a kind of rolling motion, like ocean waves, where particles move in a pattern that is almost circular. Surface waves damage structures on the surface.

Seismogram

Figure 8 The surface waves that travel along Earth's surface usually have the largest amplitudes and therefore cause the most damage.

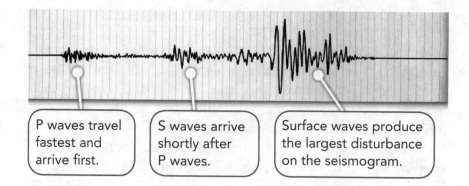

P waves travel fastest and arrive first.

S waves arrive shortly after P waves.

Surface waves produce the largest disturbance on the seismogram.

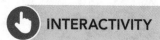

INTERACTIVITY

Analyze seismic waves to locate an earthquake.

Seismographs Seismic waves produced by earthquakes are measured by a device called a seismograph, or seismometer. This device converts the energy in the different waves to a visual called a seismogram (**Figure 8**). The seismogram shows the timing of the different seismic waves, with the relatively gentle P and S waves arriving first, followed by surface waves with larger amplitudes. The amplitudes, or heights, of the waves on a seismogram are used to quantify the size of the earthquake.

When an earthquake occurs, geologists use data from seismograph stations in different locations to pinpoint the earthquake's epicenter (**Figure 9**). Locating the epicenter helps geologists to identify areas where earthquakes may occur in the future.

READING CHECK **Determine Central Ideas** Why is it helpful for geologists to locate the epicenters of earthquakes?

....

....

Model It !

Triangulation

Figure 9 If you have data from three seismograph stations, you can locate the precise location of an earthquake's epicenter. The center of each circle is the location of a station. The radius of each circle is the distance from the epicenter. The point where the three circles overlap is the location of the epicenter.

SEP Analyze Data ✏ Draw an X on the map to indicate the epicenter of the earthquake.

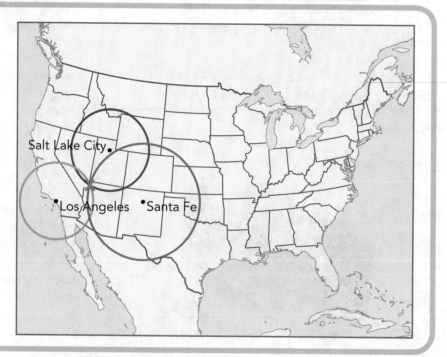

Finding an Epicenter

Geologists are trying to locate the epicenter of an earthquake. The data table below shows the arrival times of seismic waves at three different stations across Earth's surface. Use the graph to answer the questions.

Station	P Wave Arrival Time	S Wave Arrival Time	Distance from Epicenter (km)
A	4 mins, 6 s	7 mins, 25 s	
B	6 mins, 58 s	12 mins, 36 s	
C	9 mins, 21 s	16 mins, 56 s	

1. **Analyze Graphs** Use the graph to determine the distance of each station from the epicenter. Record the distances in the table.

2. **SEP Interpret Data** If another station is 5,000 km from the epicenter of the earthquake, about how long after the start of the earthquake would the S waves have arrived at this station?

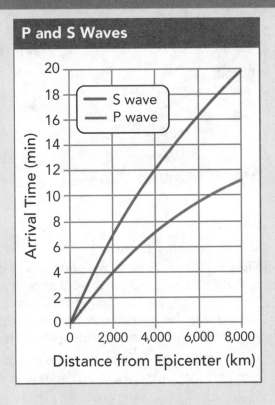

P and S Waves

Arrival Time (min) vs Distance from Epicenter (km). S wave, P wave.

Magnitude An earthquake's **magnitude** is a single number that geologists use to assign to an earthquake based on the earthquake's size. The size of an earthquake is usually measured using the moment magnitude scale, which is a measure of the energy released. Each whole-number increase in this scale represents a roughly 32-fold increase in energy. So, the seismic waves of a magnitude-9 earthquake are 10 times larger than for a magnitude-8 earthquake. The energy released, however, is 32 times greater **(Figure 10)**.

INTERACTIVITY

Explore technologies that help make buildings earthquake resistant.

Magnitude	Location	Date
9.2	Sumatra	2004
9.0	Japan	2011
7.9	China	2008
7.9	Nepal	2015
7.0	Haiti	2010

Earthquake Magnitude

Figure 10 The table shows the moment magnitudes of some large earthquakes.

CCC Scale, Proportion, and Quantity How much more energy was released by the earthquake in China than the one in Haiti?

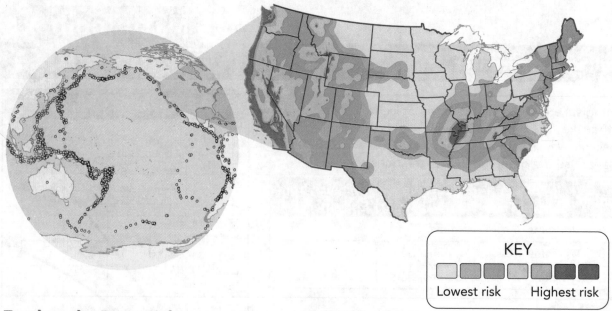

Earthquake Potential

Figure 11 The globe shows earthquakes occurring from 2007 to 2017 that were magnitude 6.0 or greater. The U.S. Geological Survey has mapped the risk of earthquakes in the United States. On the map, beige indicates the lowest risk of earthquakes occurring, while purple indicates the highest risk.

CCC Cause and Effect What do you think accounts for the higher risk of earthquakes in Los Angeles than in Chicago?

....

....

Connect to Society What societal need would wider use of technology for forecasting earthquakes address?

....

KEY

Lowest risk   Highest risk

Literacy Connection

Evaluate Media 🖊
Identify an area of the U.S. earthquake risk map in **Figure 11** that does not fit the pattern of earthquake occurrences described on this page. Circle the area.

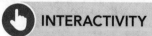

INTERACTIVITY

Help determine the best location for a new stadium in an earthquake zone.

Earthquake Risks and Tsunamis

The "Ring of Fire" around the Pacific Ocean is where many of the world's earthquakes occur. There are many plate boundaries around the Pacific, including convergent and transform boundaries where stress builds up. Because the west coast of the United States, including Alaska, is on the edge of several boundaries, the western states have a much higher risk of experiencing an earthquake than other regions of the U.S., as shown in **Figure 11**. Earthquakes themselves can cause tremendous damage, but if they occur near or below the ocean floor they can produce another type of disaster.

Ocean Floor Uplift When an area of Earth's crust moves during an earthquake, it can force anything above it to move as well. For example, an area of off-shore ocean floor that has been stressed for years at a convergent plate boundary can suddenly pop up, thrusting up the ocean water above it. Depending on how the water is moved, a tsunami may form.

A **tsunami** is a wave or series of waves produced by an earthquake or landslide. Unlike typical ocean waves formed by the wind, tsunami waves can involve the entire water column—every drop between the surface and the ocean floor—and this means they can carry tremendous energy and can be highly destructive **(Figure 12)**. In 2004, hundreds of thousands of people lost their lives due to a tsunami that struck Indonesia, Thailand, Sri Lanka, and other coastal nations around the Indian Ocean. That tsunami travelled across the Indian Ocean at a speed of 800 kilometers per hour.

Landslides
Ocean floor uplift is one cause of tsunamis. Landslides are another. In both cases, some kind of displacement of water occurs, setting the tsunami in motion. In 1958, an earthquake triggered a landslide on a mountainside on the shore of Lituya Bay, Alaska. About 30 million cubic meters of rock tumbled into the water at one end of the bay, producing a tsunami that swept across the bay and splashed as high as 524 meters up along the steep shoreline **(Figure 13)**.

☑ READING CHECK How can an earthquake or landslide produce a tsunami?

....

....

....

A Wall of Water
Figure 12 A tsunami does not always look like a wave. In some cases it is more like a sudden, massive rise in sea level, which simply floods low-lying areas.

Tsunami Hazards
Figure 13 The site of the rockslide that produced the tsunami in Lituya Bay is marked by the circle.

SEP Cite Evidence ✎
Draw lines to indicate where the water splashed up and tore away plants and sediment from the bay's shore.

☑ LESSON 3 Check

MS-ESS2-2, MS-ESS3-2

1. Identify Which type of stress on Earth's crust can make a slab of rock shorter and thicker?

....

2. SEP Construct Explanations How do mountains and valleys form through folding?

....

....

....

....

....

3. SEP Explain Phenomena You hear about a magnitude 8.0 earthquake on the news. Someone says "That doesn't sound too bad. An 8.0 is just one more than the 7.0 we had here last year." Explain why that's not the right way to think about the moment magnitude scale.

....

....

....

....

4. CCC Cause and Effect A news bulletin reports a powerful earthquake 200 kilometers off the coast of California. Hours later, there's no sign of any tsunami anywhere on the West Coast. Why not?

....

....

....

....

5. CCC Stability and Change Describe the roll that stress plays in the production of earthquakes and tsunamis.

....

....

....

....

....

....

....

....

....

Quest CHECK-INS

In this lesson, you learned about the connection between plate tectonics and features and events at Earth's surface, including mountains and earthquakes.

Evaluate How can monitoring Earth for seismic activity near plate boundaries be useful in monitoring volcanoes?

....

....

....

....

....

☝ INTERACTIVITY

Monitoring a Volcano

Go online to practice several data collection and analysis techniques to monitor a volcano and predict an eruption.

DESIGNING TO PREVENT
Destruction

▶ **VIDEO**

Watch how underwater earthquakes displace water.

How do you design buildings that can withstand the forceful waves of a tsunami? You engineer it!

The Challenge: To construct tsunami-safe buildings.

Phenomenon A seafloor earthquake can displace water above it, causing a tsunami to form. When the tsunami reaches land, giant waves cause widespread destruction.

Because parts of the United States are at risk for tsunamis, U.S. engineers have developed new building standards to save lives. They studied new design concepts. Strong columns enable buildings to stand, even when battered by tons of water and debris. Exits on upper floors allow people to get out when lower floors are flooded.

To develop standards, engineers visited Japan, where an earthquake and tsunami in 2011 caused terrible losses of life and property. The engineers also used wave research to model tsunamis and their impact on buildings.

These engineers hope that hospitals, schools, and police stations, if built to the new standards, can then provide shelter for people fleeing danger.

It is a challenge to design and engineer structures that can withstand the force of a tsunami. Under the new standards, schools would be built to withstand the force of water and debris.

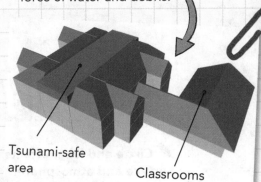

Tsunami-safe area

Classrooms

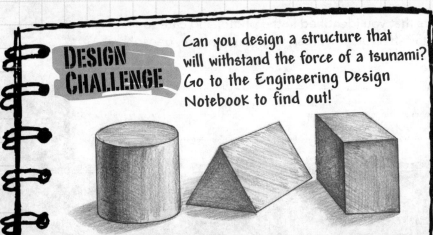

DESIGN CHALLENGE

Can you design a structure that will withstand the force of a tsunami? Go to the Engineering Design Notebook to find out!

Volcanoes and Earth's Surface

Guiding Questions

- How is plate tectonics connected to volcanic eruptions and landforms?
- What role does volcanic activity play in shaping Earth's surface?
- What hazards do different types of volcanoes pose?

Connections

Literacy Integrate With Visuals

Math Analyze Proportional Relationships

MS-ESS2-2, MS-ESS3-2

HANDS-ON LAB

uInvestigate Explore moving volcanoes.

Vocabulary

volcano
magma
lava
hot spot
extinct
dormant

Academic Vocabulary

active
composite

Connect It!

✏️ **Circle and label effects that the volcano in the photo is having on Earth's surface and atmosphere.**

CCC Systems List the effects that you identified in the photo, and categorize them by the Earth system that is affected—hydrosphere, atmosphere, geosphere, biosphere.

....

....

....

Volcanoes

While active volcanoes are found in a relatively small number of states in the U.S., they have a profound impact on Earth's surface—especially at plate boundaries. Volcanoes add new material to Earth's surface, release gases into the atmosphere, build new islands in the ocean, and shape habitats for organisms. A **volcano** is a structure that forms in Earth's crust when molten material, or magma, reaches Earth's surface. This can occur on land or on the ocean floor. **Magma** is a molten mixture of rock-forming substances, gases, and water from the mantle. Once magma reaches the surface, it is known as **lava**. When lava cools, it forms solid rock.

As with earthquakes, there is a pattern to where volcanoes occur on Earth. Most are found at convergent or divergent plate boundaries, but they can also occur at seemingly random places far from plate boundaries.

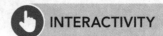

INTERACTIVITY

Explore how an erupting volcano might change Earth's surface.

Volcanism

Figure 1 The activity of volcanoes is called volcanism. Eruptions that release lava and other matter from Earth's interior can pose hazards to organisms, including humans.

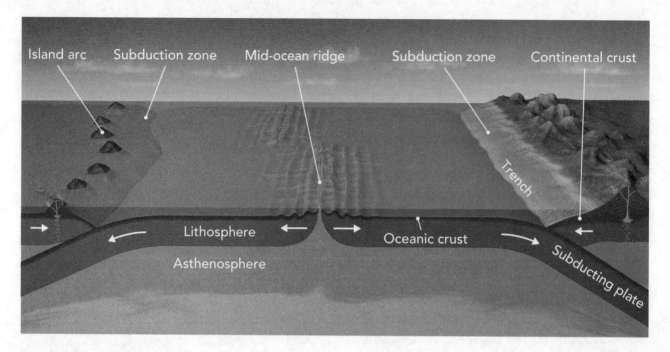

Island arc   Subduction zone   Mid-ocean ridge   Subduction zone   Continental crust

Trench

Lithosphere   Oceanic crust

Asthenosphere

Subducting plate

Divergent and Convergent Boundaries

Figure 2 Volcanic activity at plate boundaries can produce volcanoes on continents and volcanic island arcs.

SEP Construct Explanations Describe what is happening on the left side of the diagram, where ash is rising in the air over an active volcano.

....

....

....

....

....

....

....

Volcanoes and Plate Boundaries

At convergent boundaries, the subduction of an oceanic plate under a continental plate can produce volcanoes along the edge of the continent. Subduction of an oceanic plate under an adjacent oceanic plate can result in a volcanic island arc. At divergent boundaries, molten magma comes through the crust as lava, which quickly hardens into rock, but if the volume of magma is especially large, then a volcanic cone may form. **Figure 2** summarizes these processes.

At Divergent Boundaries
Volcanoes form at divergent boundaries when plates move apart and rock rises to fill the vacant space. Most volcanoes at divergent boundaries occur in the ocean at mid-ocean ridges, so they are never seen. Only in places such as Iceland can you see ocean-ridge volcanoes. Less common are volcanoes like Mt. Kilimanjaro that occur at continental divergent boundaries such as the East African Rift.

At Convergent Boundaries
When a plate dives into the mantle in the process of subduction, trapped water leaves the sinking plate and mixes with the material of the overlying mantle, causing it to melt. The buoyant magma starts to rise toward the surface. If the magma reaches the surface before cooling, a volcano forms. If the overlying plate is part of the ocean floor, the resulting volcano begins to form on the seafloor as a seamount. If it grows large enough to break the ocean surface, it becomes a volcanic island. A whole chain of islands may form when volcanism occurs at multiple spots along the edge of an oceanic plate. This is called a volcanic island arc.

HANDS-ON LAB

Investigate Explore moving volcanoes.

Hot Spot Volcanism In addition to divergent and convergent plate boundaries, there is a third source of volcanoes: hot spots. A **hot spot** is an area where lava frequently erupts at the surface, independent of plate boundary processes. Most hot spots sit atop mantle plumes of hot rock. Hot spot plumes are fixed within the deep mantle. As a plate moves over the plume, a chain of volcanoes is created because older volcanoes keep being carried away from the hot spot. The many islands and seamounts of Hawaii have formed from the westward motion of the Pacific Plate, as is illustrated in **Figure 3**. Another hot spot is found at Yellowstone National Park in Wyoming. The "supervolcano" beneath the park may erupt again someday. During past giant eruptions of Yellowstone, the last one being 640,000 years ago, most of North America was covered with volcanic ash.

▶ **VIDEO**

Learn more about volcanology.

✓ READING CHECK **Determine Conclusions** The Aleutian Islands of Alaska occur in a chain near a plate boundary. What type of boundary is it?

Model It!

Hot Spot Modeling
Figure 3 The Hawaiian Islands have formed from the movement of the Pacific Plate over a hot spot plume.

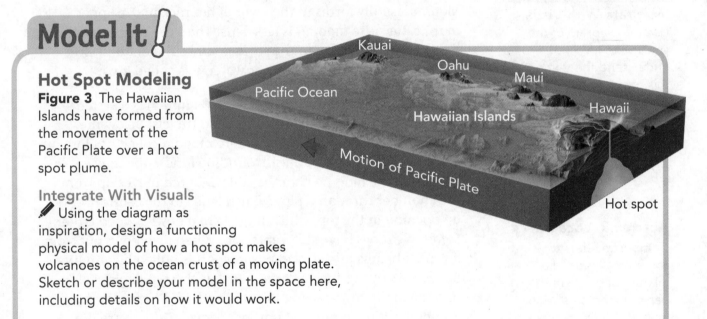

Integrate With Visuals
🖊 Using the diagram as inspiration, design a functioning physical model of how a hot spot makes volcanoes on the ocean crust of a moving plate. Sketch or describe your model in the space here, including details on how it would work.

Composite Volcano

Figure 4 A composite volcano has alternating layers of hardened lava and ash.

SEP Develop Models 🖊
Complete the diagram by reading the description of the volcano's parts and writing in the missing labels.

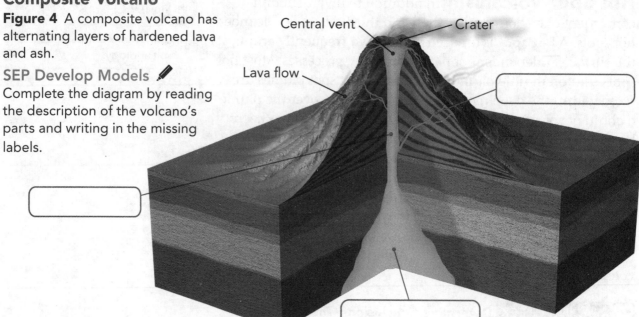

Central vent   Crater

Lava flow

Literacy Connection

Integrate With Visuals
Use the diagram of the volcano to help you understand the text on this page.

Academic Vocabulary

Composite refers to something made of a mixture of different parts or elements. Many manufactured objects are made of composites—blends of different raw materials. How does this help you to understand what a composite volcano is?

....

....

....

....

Volcano Landforms

Magma usually forms in the layer of hot rock in the upper mantle. Because magma is less dense than the rock around it, it cracks on its way up to the surface. Once the magma exits a volcano and is exposed to air or water, it is called lava.

Volcano Parts Inside a volcano (**Figure 4**) is a system of passageways through which magma travels. Below the volcano is a magma chamber, where magma collects before an eruption. The volcano and surrounding landscape may swell slightly as the magma chamber fills. Magma moves up from the chamber through a pipe, which leads to the central vent— an opening at the top, which may be in a bowl-shaped crater. Some volcanoes have side vents, too. When lava flows out from a vent, it begins to cool and harden as it is pulled by gravity down the slope of the volcano. If lava is thrown explosively into the air, it hardens and falls to Earth in different forms. Bombs are large chunks of hardened lava. Cinders are the size of pebbles. The finest particles are called ash. The type of lava-based material that emerges from a new volcano defines the type of volcano that is built.

Volcano Types The volcano in **Figure 4** is a **composite** volcano. Also called a stratovolcano, it is made of alternating layers of lava flows and ash falls. These tend to be cone-shaped and tall. Mount Fuji in Japan is an example of a composite volcano. Other types of volcanic formations are shown in **Figure 5**.

Volcanic Formations

Figure 5 Volcanic activity can result in different landforms.

1. **Compare and Contrast** How are shield volcanoes and lava plateaus similar? How are they different?

....

....

....

2. **SEP Develop Models** ✏ Review the three steps of caldera formation. Finish the sentence to describe the second phase of caldera formation.

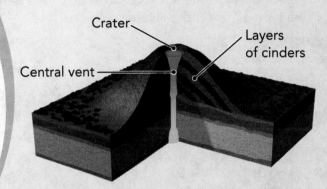

Cinder Cone Volcano If lava emerges from a new vent in Earth's crust as a mix of bombs, ash, and cinders, these materials build up into a cinder cone volcano. The loose, ashy material tends to erode quickly.

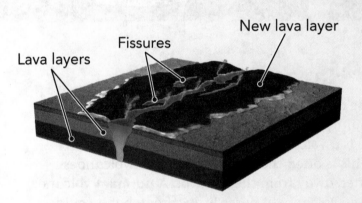

Lava Plateau Lava can flow out of several long cracks in Earth's crust and flood an area repeatedly over many years. Over time, these relatively flat layers of hardened lava build up into a lava plateau.

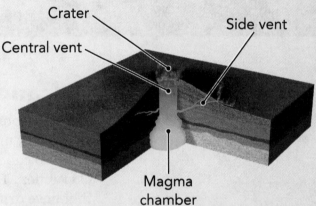

Shield Volcano Some volcanoes have slow, steady eruptions in which lava flows out and builds up over a broad area. Hot spot volcanoes tend to be shield volcanoes, and they can be massive.

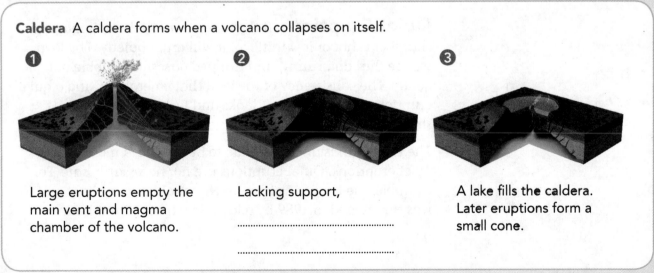

Caldera A caldera forms when a volcano collapses on itself.

1 Large eruptions empty the main vent and magma chamber of the volcano.

2 Lacking support,

....

....

3 A lake fills the caldera. Later eruptions form a small cone.

Lava from Quiet Eruptions

Figure 6 The content and consistency of lava determines the type of rock that will form as the lava cools.

INTERACTIVITY

Explore different volcanic landforms.

Academic Vocabulary

What does it mean if you have an active lifestyle?

....

....

....

Volcano Hazards

Volcanoes pose different hazards to humans and other organisms, mainly through eruptions. An **extinct**, or dead, volcano is a volcano that poses very little threat of eruption. This is often the case with hot-spot volcanoes that have drifted away from the hot spot. A **dormant** volcano is like a sleeping volcano—it poses little threat, but it could reawaken someday. **Active** volcanoes are the more immediate threat. Volcanologists classify eruptions as quiet or explosive. Whether an eruption is quiet or explosive depends in part on the magma's silica content and whether the magma is thin and runny or thick and sticky. Temperature helps determine how runny magma is.

Quiet Eruptions If the magma in a volcano's magma chamber is hot or low in silica, it will erupt quietly. The lava will be thin and runny, and trapped gases will bubble out gently. The consistency of the lava that emerges during a quiet eruption will affect how it looks and feels when it cools, as shown in **Figure 6**.

The Hawaiian Islands continue to be produced mostly by quiet eruptions. Quiet eruptions are not necessarily safe. For example, the Hawaii Volcanoes National Park's visitors center was threatened in 1989 by a lava flow from Mount Kilauea.

Explosive Eruptions

Magma that has a lot of silica will erupt more than magma containing little or no silica. High-silica magma is thick and sticky, causing it to build up in a pipe until pressure is so great that it bursts out over the surface. Trapped gases explode out instead of bubbling out gently. An explosion with that much force can hurl lava, ash, cinders, and bombs high into the atmosphere.

Krakatau, a volcano in a large volcanic arc in Indonesia, erupted in 1883. The eruption, depicted in **Figure 7**, was so violent that much of the the visible part of the island collapsed into the sea, producing a tsunami that killed 36,000 people. Gas and debris billowed more than 25 kilometers into the sky, and the sound from the explosion was heard 4,500 kilometers away. So much ash and sulfur dioxide was emitted into the atmosphere by the eruption that global temperatures were cooler for the following five years.

Krakatau Explodes

Figure 7 The eruption of Krakatau was a major disaster in Indonesia, but it affected the entire world as ash and sulfur dioxide entered the atmosphere.

Math Toolbox

Magma Composition

Magma is classified according to the amount of silica it contains. The less silica the magma contains, the more easily it flows. More silica makes magma stickier and thicker. Trapped gases can't emerge easily, so eruptions are explosive.

1. **Analyze Proportional Relationships** How do the two magma types compare in terms of silica content?

   ....

   ....

2. **SEP Construct Explanations** Which of the magma types would erupt more explosively? How would knowing the type of magma a volcano produces help nearby communities prepare for eruptions?

   ....

   ....

   ....

   ....

Types of Magma

Low-Silica

Silica 50% | Other oxides 47.5%

All other solids 2.5%

High-Silica

Silica 70% | Other oxides 27.5%

All other solids 2.5%

Measuring Gas Concentration

Figure 8 This device, called a spectrometer, can measure concentrations of volcanic gases by measuring how light passes through them. A high concentration of sulfur dioxide may mean an eruption is likely to occur.

 INTERACTIVITY

Analyze how volcanic activity can change Earth's surface.

Predicting Volcano Hazards Volcanologists use different tools to monitor volcanoes and predict eruptions. The gas emissions from volcanoes can be monitored to check for increases in sulfur dioxide, which may indicate that an eruption is coming **(Figure 8)**. Seismographs can detect rumblings deep inside a volcano that precede an eruption.

Volcanologists can also use devices to measure whether a volcano is swelling as its magma chamber fills up. These devices, called tiltmeters, are like carpenters' levels but much more sensitive. They can detect very slight changes in the tilt of a volcano's slopes. If the tilt increases, it means the volcano is swelling and likely to erupt. Telecommunications technology can transmit the data from these devices to scientists, who can then interpret the data and look for patterns associated with eruptions. They can then notify the public if an eruption is predicted.

✓ READING CHECK **Summarize Text** If the concentration of sulfur dioxide emitted from a volcano increases from less than one part per million (ppm) to 4 ppm, is the volcano more or less likely to erupt soon?

....

....

....

Question It!

Building on a Volcano

In some parts of the world, building on a volcano is a necessity because most of the land is volcanic. Suppose you had to build a home on a volcanic island.

SEP Ask Questions What questions would you want to answer before choosing a specific site for construction?

....

....

....

....

....

....

....

MS-ESS2-2, MS-ESS3-2

1. **Identify Phenomena** Runny lava oozes from the vent of a broad, gently-sloping shield volcano. What type of eruption is this?

....

2. **SEP Construct Explanations** Why do volcanoes form at divergent and convergent boundaries?

....
....
....
....
....

3. **CCC Patterns** The Hawaiian Islands formed as the Pacific Plate has moved west-northwest over a hot spot. In which part of the islands would you expect to find the most active volcanoes? What about dormant and extinct volcanoes? Explain.

....
....
....
....
....
....

4. **SEP Interpret Data** You are sailing in the South Pacific Ocean, far from any plate boundary. Looming on the horizon is a dark, broad, rounded island with sparse vegetation. A few thin flows of orange lava drip into the sea. Some smoky vapor unfurls from the center of the island. What kind of volcano is this? Explain.

....
....
....
....
....
....

5. **CCC Structure and Function** How are volcanic island arcs formed?

....
....
....
....
....
....

Quest CHECK-INS

In this lesson, you learned about the connection between plate tectonics and volcanoes.

SEP Analyze Data Why is it important to understand the type of volcano Mount Rainier is and the patterns of activity at the nearest plate boundary?

....
....
....

HANDS-ON LAB

Signs of Eruption

Go online to download the lab and identify signs of a volcanic eruption.

☑TOPIC 3 Review and Assess

① Evidence of Plate Motions

MS-ESS2-3

1. Wegener developed the hypothesis that Earth's landmasses had once been fused together, and then slowly broke apart in a process called
A. continental drift.
B. subduction.
C. Pangaea.
D. divergence.

2. Evidence that supported the hypothesis of continental drift included fossils, land features, and
A. ocean currents.
B. solar activity.
C. climate data.
D. presence of bacteria.

3. The zipper-like mountain ranges that run across the floors of the ocean are called
A. tectonic plates.
B. mid-ocean ridges.
C. subduction zones.
D. convergent boundaries.

4. SEP Develop Models 🖊 In the space below, sketch one of the types of stress that affect Earth's crust.

② Plate Tectonics and Earth's Surface

MS-ESS2-2

5. Which of the following explains how Mount Everest formed?
A. The mountain formed from volcanic activity at a divergent boundary.
B. The mountain formed when two tectonic plates collided at a convergent boundary.
C. The mountain formed from volcanic activity at a convergent boundary.
D. The mountain formed as a result of an earthquake when two plates slipped past each other.

6. The circular movement of material in the mantle that drives plate movement is called
A. conduction.
B. subduction.
C. compression.
D. convection.

7. Plates move apart from each other at a
A. divergent boundary.
B. convergent boundary.
C. transform boundary.
D. subduction boundary.

8. Earthquakes often occur along
.... as a result of the buildup of stress.

9. SEP Construct Explanations A local official pledges to have a new highway built over a transform boundary. Explain why this may be a bad idea.

....

....

....

....

....

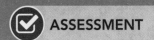

3 Earthquakes and Tsunami Hazards

MS-ESS2-2, MS-ESS3-2

10. The type of stress that pulls on and thins an area of Earth's crust is called
A. torsion.
B. tension.
C. shearing.
D. diverging.

11. When a plate is compressed, it can create anticlines and synclines that can become
A. mountains and valleys.
B. folds and breaks.
C. plateaus and canyons.
D. landmasses and oceans.

12. How much more energy is released by an earthquake with a magnitude of 8.0 on the moment magnitude scale than one with a 6.0 magnitude?
A. 32 times more
B. 64 times more
C. 2 times more
D. 20 times more

13. SEP Explain Phenomena Describe how ocean floor uplift and landslides can cause tsunamis.

....

....

....

....

....

....

....

4 Volcanoes and Earth's Surface

MS-ESS2-2, MS-ESS3-2

14. Volcanoes may emerge at long cracks in Earth's crust at .... ridges, on continents near convergent ...., and at random locations away from plate boundaries called ....

15. SEP Construct Explanations What causes volcanoes to form along a mid-ocean ridge?

....

....

....

....

....

16. CCC Cause and Effect Why are volcanoes often found along both convergent and divergent plate boundaries?

....

....

....

....

....

....

....

....

....

143

Evidence-Based Assessment

MS-ESS2-2, MS-ESS3-2

In 2011, a magnitude 9.0 earthquake occurred in the ocean floor off the east coast of Japan. Tsunameter buoys and tide gauges recorded tsunami waves as they crossed the Pacific Ocean. Scientists used the data to predict how large the waves would be and when they would arrive at different locations. The map shown represents the tsunami forecast model for the event, which was used by coastal communities around the Pacific to prepare for local impacts of the tsunami.

Analyze the map of the 2011 tsunami wave forecast. Keep in mind the following information:

- The triangles symbolize specific tsunameter buoys, which measure wave height, or amplitude.

- The numbered contour lines represent how many hours after the earthquake the tsunami waves were forecasted to reach those areas of the ocean.

- Major plate boundaries are are indicated on the map.

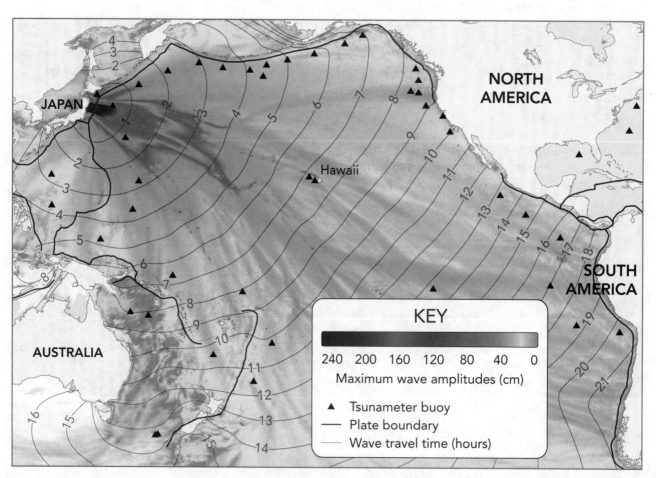

1. **SEP Analyze Data** According to the data, where was tsunami wave height expected to be greatest?
   - **A.** Australia
   - **B.** Japan
   - **C.** North America
   - **D.** South America

2. **SEP Interpret Data** How many hours after the earthquake were the tsunami waves expected to reach South America?
   - **A.** 9
   - **B.** 23
   - **C.** 7
   - **D.** 19

3. **Model Phenomena** When was a tsunami wave expected to reach Hawaii, and what was the expected wave height?

   ....
   ....
   ....
   ....
   ....
   ....
   ....
   ....
   ....

4. **CCC Cause and Effect** Describe how the motion of tectonic plates can result in a tsunami.

   ....
   ....
   ....
   ....
   ....
   ....
   ....
   ....

5. **SEP Construct Explanations** In terms of their usefulness in protecting human lives, why are so many tsunameters placed along coastlines of the Pacific Ocean? Provide two explanations.

   ....
   ....
   ....
   ....
   ....
   ....
   ....
   ....
   ....
   ....
   ....
   ....

Quest FINDINGS

Complete the Quest!

Phenomenon Present information on Mount Rainier's history and current geological research, along with your evidence-based argument about whether it is safe to hike and camp there.

SEP Reason Quantitatively What data will help you to predict that Mount Rainier could erupt while you are on a two-week camping trip nearby? Explain.

....
....
....

▶ **INTERACTIVITY**

Reflect on Mount Rainier's Safety

MS-ESS2-2, MS-ESS3-2

Modeling Sea-Floor Spreading

How can you prevent a major oil spill by **designing** and building a model that **demonstrates** sea-floor spreading?

Background

Phenomenon Imagine you are a marine geologist reviewing a plan to construct a gas pipeline attached to the ocean floor. You notice that part of the pipeline will cross a mid-ocean ridge zone. In this investigation, you will design and build a model that demonstrates sea-floor spreading to show why this plan is not a good idea.

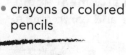
Materials

(per group)
- scissors
- transparent tape
- colored marker
- metric ruler
- 2 sheets of unlined letter-sized paper
- manila folder or file
- crayons or colored pencils

Safety

Be sure to follow all safety guidelines provided by your teacher. The Safety Appendix of your textbook provides more details about the safety icons.

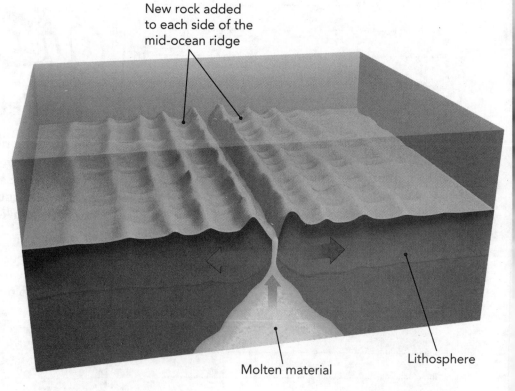

New rock added to each side of the mid-ocean ridge

Molten material

Lithosphere

Design Your Model and Investigation

Discuss with your group why building a pipeline that spans the mid-ocean ridge is a bad idea. Over time, what will happen to the pipeline?

With your group, take a look at the materials. How can you use the materials to construct a model that demonstrates why the pipeline plan is a problem?

HANDS-ON LAB

и**Demonstrate** Go online for a downloadable worksheet of this lab.

Consider the following questions:

- How can you use the manila folder to represent the mantle?

- How can you use the two pieces of plain letter-sized paper to create matching strips of striped sea floor?

- How can you represent the mid-ocean ridge and the subduction zones on either side of the ridge?

Use the space provided to sketch your group's model and write notes for guiding its construction. Have your teacher approve your group's plan, and then construct and demonstrate the model.

Sketch of Model

Design Notes

Analyze and Interpret Data

1. **SEP Develop Models** Why is it important that your model have identical patterns of stripes on both sides of the center slit?

   ....

   ....

   ....

   ....

2. **SEP Construct Explanations** Use evidence from your model to support the claim that sea-floor spreading builds two different tectonic plates.

   ....

   ....

   ....

   ....

3. **SEP Refine Your Solution** Look at the models created by other groups. How are the other solutions different? How might you revise your group's model to better demonstrate sea-floor spreading?

   ....

   ....

   ....

   ....

4. **SEP Use Models** How could your group revise the model to reinforce the idea that the amount of crust that forms at the mid-ocean ridge is equal to the amount of crust recycled back into the mantle at subduction zones?

   ....

   ....

   ....

   ....

5. **CCC Stability and Change** How does your model support the claim that building an oil pipeline across a divergent boundary would be a bad idea?

   ....

   ....

   ....

NGSS PERFORMANCE EXPECTATION

MS-ESS1-4 Construct a scientific explanation based on evidence from rock strata for how the geologic time scale is used to organize Earth's 4.6-billion-year-old history.

HANDS-ON LAB

uConnect Develop a timeline of the major events in the life of a family member.

What do these
fossils reveal about
Earth's past?

GO ONLINE
to access your
digital course

▶ VIDEO

👆 INTERACTIVITY

🧪 VIRTUAL LAB

☑ ASSESSMENT

📖 eTEXT

🧪 HANDS-ON LABS

The Essential Question

How can events in Earth's past be organized?

CCC Stability and Change Earth has changed a lot since these ammonites swam the ocean. Our planet has changed even more since it first formed. How do scientists find out about events in Earth's history? Identify several things that you think scientists study to find out how Earth has changed over time.

....

....

....

....

....

Quest KICKOFF

How do paleontologists know where to look for fossils?

Phenomenon Dr. Digg is the head paleontologist at a museum. She has hired you to help the museum set up a new exhibit on an extinct genus of ancient animal called *Dimetrodon*. Where in the world can you find *Dimetrodon* fossils to form the centerpiece of the exhibit? Fossils are found all over Earth, and you can't dig up the entire planet. In this problem-based Quest activity, you will choose a dig site that is likely to produce fossils of *Dimetrodon*. You will evaluate information about four sites, using information about rock layers and other fossils found at those sites to narrow the choices down. In a final report, you will share your evaluations of each site and give reasons for choosing one site and rejecting the other three.

NBC LEARN ▶ VIDEO

After viewing the Quest Kickoff video and watching a paleontologist at work, complete the concept map by recording four things that you should consider when exploring for fossils.

How to Find Fossils

INTERACTIVITY

The Big Fossil Hunt

MS-ESS1-4 Construct a scientific explanation based on evidence from rock strata for how the geologic time scale is used to organize Earth's 4.6-billion-year-old history.

Quest CHECK-INS

IN LESSON 1

What do paleontologists learn from layers of rock and the organisms found within those layers? Gather clues to find the best dig site.

INTERACTIVITY

Clues in the Rock Layers

INTERACTIVITY

Fossils Around the World

Quest CHECK-IN

IN LESSON 2

How do paleontologists use the geologic time scale to help find fossils? Explore how scientists use information from already-discovered fossils to predict where other fossils might be.

HANDS-ON LAB

A Matter of Time

The Carnegie Dinosaur Quarry is a dig site within the Dinosaur National Monument in Utah. Paleontologists excavate and preserve dinosaur fossils that range from 148 to 155 million years old.

Quest CHECK-IN

IN LESSON 3

How do paleontologists use information about ancient organisms to determine where to search for fossils? Conduct research and make a final selection of a dig site for *Dimetrodon*.

 INTERACTIVITY

Time to Choose the Dig Site

Quest FINDINGS

Complete the Quest!

Prepare a report in which you evaluate each site and give reasons for choosing or rejecting that site.

 INTERACTIVITY

Reflect on the Big Fossil Hunt

Dividing History

How can you use a timeline of a person's life as a **model** of Earth's history?

Background

Phenomenon A person's life can be divided into segments based on achievements or other notable events. In this activity, you will divide a family member's life into blocks of time and compare this to how geologic time is divided.

Develop a Model

1. Choose a member of your family or another important person in your life.

2. Interview the person you chose. Select what information you will record in the Observations section, such as his or her career, family life, personal achievements, and so on. As you record your data, be sure to note dates and important names, such as the names of spouses and children.

3. Divide the person's life into at least three separate segments based on criteria that you choose.

4. Use the materials to make a timeline of the person's life. Record important events and accomplishments during each of the segments of time.

5. Exchange your timeline with another student. Discuss the timelines and how they were constructed.

Materials

(per individual)

- sheet of plain white paper (or your lab journal or science notebook)
- metric ruler

Observations

HANDS-ON LAB

☑**Connect** Go online for a downloadable worksheet of this lab.

Analyze and Conclude

1. **SEP Develop Models** Who did you choose, and what types of criteria did you use to divide his or her life into blocks of time?

   ....

   ....

   ....

   ....

2. **Determine Differences** Do you agree or disagree with how the timeline you received from the other student is divided? Explain.

   ....

   ....

3. **SEP Use Models** Why is it important to establish the criteria on which a time scale will be based?

   ....

   ....

   ....

4. **CCC Evaluate Scale** What might a timeline of the history of Earth look like and how could it be divided into sections? Consider the timeline you constructed. What are the advantages and limitations of your timeline as a model for Earth's history? Make sure to account for the time scale of your model.

   ....

   ....

   ....

   ....

Determining Ages of Rocks

Guiding Questions

- How do geologists describe the ages of rocks?
- How do geologists determine the relative ages of rocks?
- How do geologists determine the absolute ages of rocks?

Connections

Literacy Write Explanatory Texts

Math Write an Expression

MS-ESS1-4

HANDS-ON LAB

μ**Investigate** Model changes in rocks.

Vocabulary

relative age
absolute age
law of
  superposition
fossil
unconformity
radioactive decay
radioactive dating

Academic Vocabulary

relative
infer

Connect It!

✎ **How many rock layers do you see? Draw an arrow pointing from the youngest rock to the oldest rock.**

SEP Construct Explanations How did you decide which rocks are the youngest and oldest?

....

....

....

SEP Plan and Carry Out Investigations Suppose you were the first person to study the canyon. How could you find out exactly how old the oldest rock is?

....

....

....

Describing the Ages of Rocks

If you visit the Painted Desert in Arizona, you will find rock layers that look grey, red, green, blue, and even purple. If you're curious, you might start by asking "How did these colorful rocks form?" Your next question would probably be "How old are these rocks?" In other words, you would want to describe the ages of the rocks. Geologists have two ways to describe the age of a rock: age **relative** to another rock and age in number of years since the rock formed.

Relative Age

The **relative age** of a rock is its age compared to the ages of other rocks. You probably use the idea of relative age when you compare your age with someone else's. For example, if you say that you are older than your brother but younger than your sister, you describe your relative age.

Absolute Age

The relative age of a rock does not provide its absolute age. The **absolute age** of a rock is the number of years that have passed since the rock formed. It may be impossible to know the exact absolute age of some rocks, so geologists often use both absolute and relative ages.

Why do geologists want to analyze and describe the ages of rocks? Evidence of past events occurs in rocks. That evidence shows that Earth has changed and evolved over time due to natural processes. Rock layers like those in **Figure 1** form a record of Earth's history of change, known as the geologic record. By studying clues in Earth's rocks and determining their ages, geologist can organize past events in sequence to better understand Earth's history.

✔ READING CHECK **Summarize** What is the difference between relative age and absolute age?

....

....

....

Academic Vocabulary

Describe your location relative to an object or another person in the room.

....

....

....

Rainbow of Rock Layers

Figure 1 Many colorful rock layers make up the hills of Arizona's Painted Desert. These rock layers represent many millions of years of Earth's history.

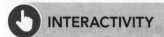

Examine a sequence of rock layers to learn their relative ages.

Determining Relative Ages of Rocks

Geologists use many methods to determine the age of Earth's rocks. To find a rock's relative age, they analyze the position of rock layers. They also look for a variety of clues in rocks, such as fossils. These methods provide ways to find relative ages, but not absolute ages, of rocks.

Clues Within Rocks

Figure 2 Intrusions and faults can help to determine a sequence of events within rock layers.

1. **Identify Knowns**
   ✎ Draw an X over the igneous intrusion.
   Draw a line along a fault.

2. **CCC Patterns** ✎
   The rock layers are (older / younger) than any faults or intrusions that run through them.

3. **Synthesize Information** The San Andreas fault runs for hundreds of miles through California. What occurs when rocks on either side of the fault move?

Position of Rock Layers Sedimentary rock usually forms in horizontal layers, or strata. Geologists use the **law of superposition** to determine the relative ages of sedimentary rock layers. According to the law of superposition, in undisturbed horizontal sedimentary rock layers, the oldest layer is at the bottom and the youngest layer is at the top. The higher you go, the younger the rocks are. The lower or deeper you go, the older the rocks are.

Clues from Igneous Rocks Magma is molten material beneath Earth's surface. Lava (magma that reaches the surface) can harden on the surface to form an igneous extrusion. Magma can also push into layers of rock below the surface. The magma can harden and form an igneous intrusion, like the one shown in **Figure 2**. An extrusion is younger than the rock it covers. An intrusion is younger than the rock around it.

Clues from Faults More clues come from the study of faults. A fault, like the one shown in **Figure 2**, is a break in Earth's crust. Forces inside Earth cause movement of the rock on opposite sides of a fault. A fault is always younger than the rock it cuts through. To determine the relative age of a fault, geologists find the relative age of the youngest layer cut by the fault.

Igneous Intrusion

Faults

Using Fossils The preserved remains or traces of living things are called **fossils**. They most often occur in layers of sedimentary rock. Fossils preserved in rock layers provide physical evidence about the history of life on Earth and how Earth has changed over time.

Certain fossils, called index fossils, help geologists to match and date rock layers, even if those layers are far apart or in different locations. An index fossil is a fossil of an organism that was widely distributed and existed for a geologically short period of time. Fossils from organisms that lived for a long geologic time might show up in multiple rock layers, but index fossils show up in only a few layers. Index fossils are useful because they tell the relative ages of the rock layers in which they occur. Geologists **infer** that layers with matching index fossils are the same age.

You can use index fossils to match rock layers and find their relative age. Look at the diagram in **Figure 3,** which shows rock layers from four different locations. Notice that two of the fossils are found in only one rock layer. These are index fossils.

INTERACTIVITY

Use index fossils to decode Earth's history.

Academic Vocabulary

Think about a pet you saw recently. What can you infer about the animal's age? Explain your answer.

....

....

....

....

Model It !

Using Fossils to Match Rock Layers

Figure 3 You can model how scientists use index fossils to match rock layers separated by distance.

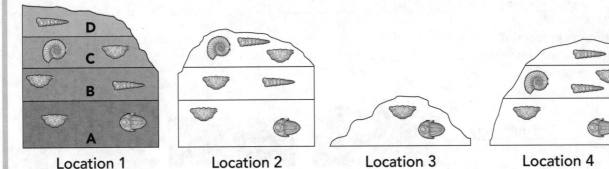

Location 1   Location 2   Location 3   Location 4

1. **Interpret Diagrams** ✏ At Location 1, circle the fossils that you can use as index fossils.

2. **SEP Use Models** ✏ Use the index fossils at Location 1 to label the matching layers at Locations 2–4. Then, draw a line to connect each matching layer across all locations and shade them the same color.

3. **CCC Patterns** At Location 4, what can you infer about the ages of rocks and history? Cite evidence to support your inference.

....

....

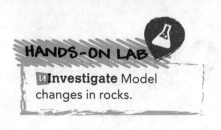
Literacy Connection

Write Explanatory Texts Underline the sentences in the text that explain how the rock layers in **Figure 4** changed.

Unconformity and Folding

Figure 4 🖊 Shade the oldest and youngest layers in the last two diagrams. Label the unconformity. Circle the part of the fold that is overturned.

Changes in Rocks The geologic record of sedimentary rock layers is not complete. In fact, erosion destroyed most of Earth's geologic record over billions of years. Gaps in the geologic record and folding can change the position in which rock layers appear. As was shown in **Figure 2**, motion along faults can also change how rock layers line up. These changes make it harder for scientists to reconstruct Earth's history. **Figure 4** shows how the order of rock layers may change.

Gaps in the Geologic Record When rock layers erode, an older rock surface may be exposed. Then deposition begins again, building new rock layers. The surface where new rock layers meet a much older rock surface beneath them is called an unconformity. An **unconformity** is a gap in the geologic record. It shows where rock layers have been lost due to erosion.

Folding Sometimes, forces inside Earth fold rock layers so much that the layers are turned over completely. In this case, the youngest rock layers may be on the bottom!

Samples from many different areas are needed to give a complete geologic record. Geologists compare rock layers in many places to understand a complete sequence.

✓ READING CHECK **Write Explanatory Texts** In you own words, explain one of the methods that geologists use to find the relative ages of rocks.

....

....

....

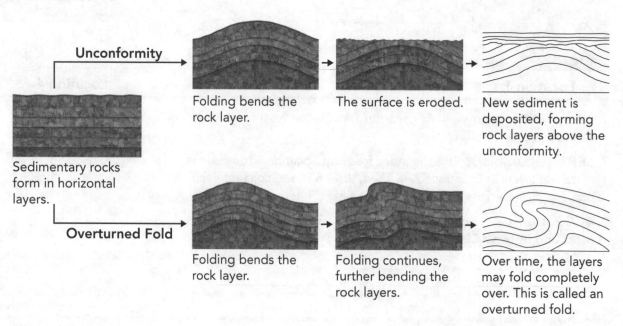

Unconformity

Sedimentary rocks form in horizontal layers.

Folding bends the rock layer.

The surface is eroded.

New sediment is deposited, forming rock layers above the unconformity.

Overturned Fold

Folding bends the rock layer.

Folding continues, further bending the rock layers.

Over time, the layers may fold completely over. This is called an overturned fold.

Determining Absolute Ages of Rocks

Geologist use different methods to determine the absolute age of Earth's rocks. To find a rock's absolute age, they use certain elements in rocks that change over time.

Radioactive Decay An element is said to be radioactive when its particles become unstable and release energy in the form of radiation. This process is called radioactive decay. During **radioactive decay**, the atoms of one element break down to form atoms of another element.

Radioactive elements occur naturally in some igneous rocks. As an unstable radioactive element decays, it slowly changes into a stable element. The amount of the radioactive element decreases, but the amount of the new element increases, causing the overall composition of elements in the rock to change.

Each radioactive element decays at its own constant rate, represented by its half-life. The half-life of a radioactive element measures the time it takes for half of the radioactive atoms to decay. You can see in **Figure 5** how a radioactive element decays over time. Scientists use the half-life ratio to calculate the age of the rock in which a radioactive element is found.

Reflect Think about rocks you have collected, or buildings, statues, or landforms made of rock that you have seen. For which rock would you like to find the absolute age? Record this in your science notebook.

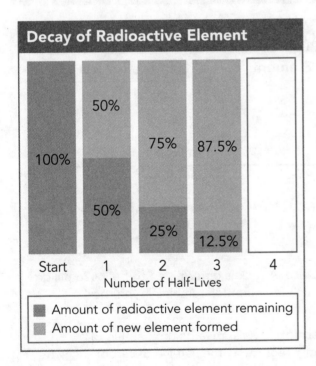

Decay of Radioactive Element

100%
50% 50%
75% 25%
87.5% 12.5%

Start 1 2 3 4
Number of Half-Lives

■ Amount of radioactive element remaining
■ Amount of new element formed

Radioactive Decay and Half-Life
Figure 5 This is a sample element that illustrates radioactive decay.

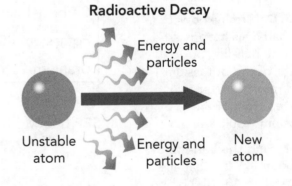

Radioactive Decay

Energy and particles

Unstable atom → New atom

Energy and particles

1. **CCC Patterns** 🖊 What pattern do you see in the graph? Use the pattern to complete the last bar.

2. **CCC Scale, Proportion, and Quantity** 🖊 The graph shows that as the amount of the old radioactive element (increases/decreases), the amount of the new stable element (increases/decreases).

INTERACTIVITY

Use radioactive dating to determine the absolute age of different objects.

Radioactive Dating

Geologists use **radioactive dating**, or radiometric dating, to determine the absolute ages of rocks. In radioactive dating, scientists first determine the amount of a radioactive element in a rock sample. Then they compare that with the amount of the stable element into which the radioactive element decays. They use this information and the half-life of the element to calculate the age of the rock.

Potassium-Argon Dating Scientists often date rocks using potassium-40. This form of potassium decays to stable argon-40 and has a half-life of 1.3 billion years. Potassium-40 is useful in dating the most ancient rocks because of its long half-life.

Carbon-14 Dating Scientists can date plant and animal remains using carbon-14. All organisms contain carbon, including this radioactive form. Carbon-14 decays to stable nitrogen-14 and has a half-life of only 5,730 years. Therefore, this method can't be used to date remains older than about 50,000 years because the amount of carbon-14 left would be too small to measure accurately.

READING CHECK

Determine Central Ideas Underline the main idea in the first paragraph.

Math Toolbox

Using Radioactive Dating to Calculate Absolute Age

A rock contains 25 percent of the potassium-40 it started with. Use radioactive dating to calculate the absolute age.

Step 1. Determine how many half-lives have passed. After one half-life, 50 percent of the potassium would remain. After two half-lives, 25% of the potassium would remain.

Step 2. Find the half-life of potassium-40. The half-life of potassium-40 is 1.3 billion years.

Step 3. Multiply the half-life by the number of half-lives that have passed to calculate the rock's age. 1.3 billion years × 2 half-lives = 2.6 billion years old.

Elements Used in Radioactive Dating	
Radioactive Element	**Half-life (years)**
Carbon-14	5,730
Potassium-40	1.3 billion
Uranium-235	713 million

1. **SEP Use Mathematics** A bone contains 12.5 percent of the carbon-14 it began with. How old is the bone?

....

2. **SEP Interpret Data** A rock is determined to be 1.426 billion years old. How much uranium-235 remains in the rock?

....

3. **Write an Expression** If X represents the half-life of potassium–40 and Y represents the half-life of carbon-14, write an expression that correctly compares the two half-lives.

....

☑ LESSON 1 Check

1. **Identify** What method do geologists use to find the absolute ages of rocks?

....

....

2. **Explain** How could a geologist match the rock layers in one area to rock layers found in another area?

....

....

....

....

....

3. **CCC Patterns** A layer of sandstone sits above two other layers of rock. A fault cuts through the two lower layers of rock. How does the age of the fault compare with the ages of all three rock layers?

....

....

....

....

4. **SEP Construct Explanations** A geologist observes rock layers that are folded. She determines that a layer of siltstone is younger than the layer of limestone above it. How can you explain the geologist's findings?

....

....

....

....

....

5. **Apply Scientific Reasoning** A scientist finds tools made of rock in the ruins of an ancient home. He also finds burned wood likely cut by the tools in the home's fire pit. How could the scientist estimate when the tools were made?

....

....

....

....

Quest CHECK-INS

In this lesson, you learned how geologists find the ages of rocks and how events and fossil histories are recorded within the rock layers.

Explain How can information from rock layers give you clues about where to look for additional fossils?

....

....

....

....

....

👆 INTERACTIVITIES

- Clues in the Rock Layers
- Fossils Around the World

Go online to think about the layers of rock at the dig sites and to consider how knowing more about the ages of rocks and fossils can help you to choose where to look for another fossil.

MS-ESS1-4

REWRITING THE HISTORY OF
Your Food

Modern tomatillos

If you have ever eaten salsa verde with your tacos, then you have likely eaten a tomatillo (toh mah TEE yoh). Related to husk tomatoes and ground cherries, modern tomatillos have a paper-thin husk covering their berry-shaped fruit.

Tomatillos are members of the plant genus *Physalis*, a small part of the nightshade family. This family includes many plants that we eat, including peppers, eggplants, and potatoes, and some too dangerous to eat, such as the poisonous belladonna plant.

Until recently, the evolution of these plants was poorly understood. Because many parts of the plants decompose easily, the fossil record is limited. Based on those limited fossils, scientists inferred that plants similar to tomatillos and ground cherries evolved fairly recently, about 9 to 11 million years ago.

However, scientist rewrote the tomatillo's history with a recent discovery from Patagonia, a region that covers southern Argentina and Chile. An international team collected thousands of fossils to study the evolutionary relationship between extinct and living organisms. Among the samples, they found two fossils of husked fruit, ancestors of the modern tomatillo.

The fossils were preserved in sediment deposited in an ancient lake near a volcano. Based on radioactive, or radiometric, dating of volcanic rocks found with the fossils, scientists concluded that ancestral tomatillos are actually more than 50 million years old! These plants existed in southern South America when the region was close to Antarctica and had a warm and wet climate—very different from its modern dry, cool climate. So enjoy some salsa verde and appreciate just how long the ancestors of those tomatillos have been growing on Earth!

Fossil Location in South America

fossil location

Patagonia

Tomatillo Group Fossil Record

	Previously-Discovered Fossils	Newly-Discovered Fossils
Plant Parts Preserved	Tiny seeds and wood	Husks and fruit
Approximate Age	9 to 11 million years old	52 million years old
Dating Method Used	Molecular dating (uses rates of change and DNA to determine when organisms evolved) based on modern plants and fossils	Argon-argon dating (a newer variation of potassium-argon dating) of volcanic rocks found with the fossils

Use the text and table to answer the following questions.

1. **CCC Scale, Proportion, and Quantity** Based on new data, what conclusion did scientists draw about the tomatillo and nightshade plant family?

2. **SEP Use Mathematics** About how much older are the newly-discovered plant fossils compared to the age of previously discovered fossils?

3. **SEP Evaluate Information** What evidence supports the scientists' conclusion about the age of the husk fruits and the nightshade family overall?

4. **SEP Construct Explanations** How has radioactive dating helped to change our understanding of Earth's history? Use evidence from the fossil discovery to support your answer.

② Geologic Time Scale

Guiding Questions

- What is the purpose of the geologic time scale?
- How do events help geologists define and divide geologic time?

Connection

Literacy Write Informative Texts

MS-ESS1-4

HANDS-ON LAB

uInvestigate Model the geologic time scale.

Vocabulary

geologic time
  scale
era
period

Academic Vocabulary

organize
refine

Connect It !

✏ **Circle the unconformity. What does it tell you about the history of this location?**

SEP Analyze and Interpret Data What can you infer about the history based on these rocks?

....

....

....

Explain How could you use the information in these rocks to organize events in Earth's history?

....

....

....

The Geologic Time Scale

When you speak of the past, what names do you use for different spans of time? You probably use names such as century, decade, year, month, week, and day. But these units aren't very helpful for thinking about much longer periods of time—such as the 4.6 billion years of Earth's history.

To **organize** this vast number of years into manageable periods, scientists created the geologic time scale. The **geologic time scale** is a record of the geologic events and the evolution of life forms as shown in the rock and fossil records. Notice that it is a timeline—a model of the relative order of events over a long period of time that might otherwise be difficult to study.

Scientists first developed the geologic time scale by studying rock layers and index fossils worldwide. They gathered evidence using methods of determining the relative ages of rocks, such as evidence from unconformities as in **Figure 1**. With this evidence, scientists placed Earth's rocks in order by relative age. Later, they used radioactive dating to help them determine the absolute age of the divisions in the geologic time scale.

☑ READING CHECK **Summarize Text** How do scientists organize Earth's history and what evidence do they use?

....

....

....

VIDEO

Consider the best way to represent the geologic time scale.

Academic Vocabulary

Describe how you organize something in your life. Compare the state of that thing before and after you organized it.

....

....

....

....

....

....

A Gap in Time

Figure 1 This unconformity represents a gap in geologic time of about 65 million years. The remaining rocks tell the story of how Earth evolved over geologic time.

The Geologic Time Scale

Figure 2 The geologic time scale is based on physical evidence from rock and fossil records that show how Earth has evolved over geologic time. The divisions of the geologic time scale are used to organize events in Earth's history.

1. **Calculate** 🖊 After you read the rest of the lesson, calculate and fill in the duration of each period.

2. **CCC Evaluate Scale** 🖊 Use the time scale to identify the period in which each organism pictured below lived.

3. **SEP Develop Models** 🖊 Draw lines from each fossil or rock pictured on the right to the part of the time scale that represents when it formed.

Precambrian Time

Paleozoic Era

Period		Cambrian	Ordovician	Silurian	Devonian	Carboniferous	
Began (Millions of Years Ago)	4,600	541	485	444	419	359	
Duration (Millions of Years)	4,059	....	41	25	60	....	

Organism: *Velociraptor*
Age: about 80 million years
Period: ....

Organism: *Wiwaxia*
Age: about 500 million years
Period: ....

► Limestone and shale containing fossil coral from Kentucky and Indiana provide evidence that a shallow sea covered much of North America during the Silurian period.

▼ Geologic evidence such as these deposits from an ancient glacial lake in Washington suggest that a period of major global cooling began about 2.6 million years ago.

◄ Fossilized cyanobacteria that date to about 3.5 billion years ago provide evidence that single-celled organisms actually appeared during the Precambrian.

Mesozoic Era

Cenozoic Era

	Permian		Triassic	Jurassic	Cretaceous		Paleogene	Neogene	Quarternary
	299		252	201	145		66	23	2.6
				56	79			20.4	2.6
	....		....				....		

Organism: *Smilodon*

Age: between about 2.5 million and 10,000 years

Period: ....

167

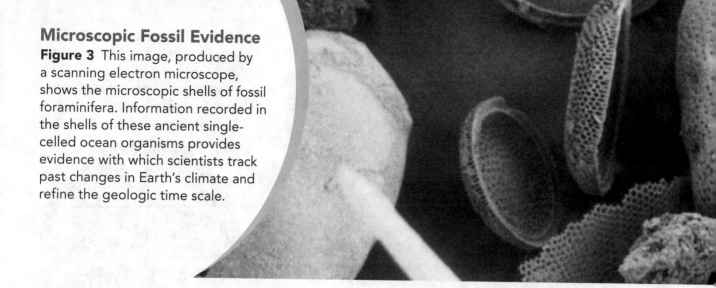

Microscopic Fossil Evidence
Figure 3 This image, produced by a scanning electron microscope, shows the microscopic shells of fossil foraminifera. Information recorded in the shells of these ancient single-celled ocean organisms provides evidence with which scientists track past changes in Earth's climate and refine the geologic time scale.

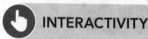

INTERACTIVITY

Review how geologists learn about Earth's history.

HANDS-ON LAB

ᴎ**Investigate** Model the geologic time scale.

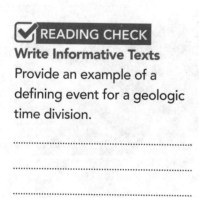

READING CHECK

Write Informative Texts
Provide an example of a defining event for a geologic time division.

....

....

....

Dividing Geologic Time

As geologists studied the rock and fossil records, they found major changes in life forms at certain times. Fossils are widely distributed in Earth's rocks. They occur in rocks in a definite order, with new species appearing and old species disappearing. In this way, fossils provided evidence of change on Earth. Geologists used these changes to help identify major events in Earth's history and mark where one unit of geologic time ends and the next begins. Therefore, most divisions of the geologic time scale depend on events in the history of life on Earth. **Figure 2** shows the major divisions of the geologic time scale.

Precambrian Time Geologic time begins with a long span of time called Precambrian (pree KAM bree un) time. Precambrian time covers about 88 percent of Earth's history, from 4.6 billion years ago to 541 million years ago. Few fossils survive from this time period.

Eras Geologists divide the time between the Precambrian and the present into three long units of time called **eras**. During the Paleozoic era, life increased in complexity and Pangaea formed. The Mesozoic era is defined by the dominance of dinosaurs and Pangaea breaking apart. During the Cenozoic era, mammals evolved to become the dominant land animals and the continents moved to their present-day positions.

Periods Eras are subdivided into units of geologic time called **periods**. You can see in **Figure 2** that the Mesozoic era includes three periods: the Triassic period, the Jurassic period, and the Cretaceous period. Each period is defined by certain events. For example, at the end of the Cretaceous period, major volcanic eruptions coincided with the impact on Earth of a huge asteroid. These events significantly changed the global environment.

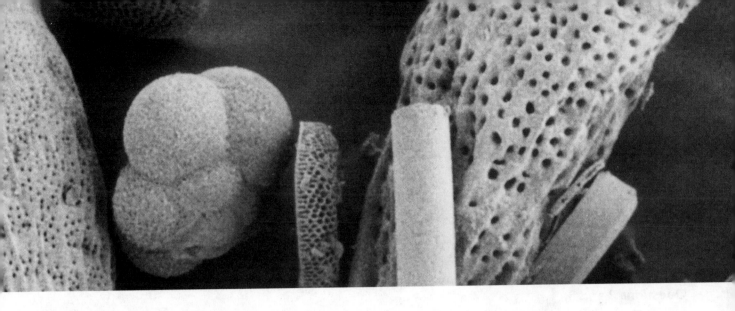

Refining Earth's History

Our understanding of Earth's history changes with each newly-discovered fossil (see **Figure 3**) or rock. Our understanding also changes as the technology used to analyze rocks and fossils advances. That's why geologists continually **refine** the geologic time scale. For example, geologists use the start of a period of major global cooling to mark the beginning of the Quaternary period. Recently, evidence from ocean floor sediments and other sources led scientists to move that boundary from 1.8 to 2.6 million years ago. The new boundary, based on new physical evidence, more accurately reflects a major change in Earth's climate.

Academic Vocabulary
Describe how you might refine something you make or do.

....

....

....

....

Literacy Connection

Write Informative Texts
After you read this page, explain in your own words why scientists constantly refine the geologic time scale.

....

....

....

....

....

....

Question It!

Modeling Geologic Time

Suppose your friend makes his own model of the geologic time scale. He decided to use a scale of 1 m = 1 million years. Would your friend's model work?

1. **CCC Scale, Proportion, and Quantity** How would your friend's model differ from the geologic time scale shown in **Figure 2**?

....

....

2. **SEP Develop Models** What would be one advantage and one disadvantage of your friend's model?

....

....

....

....

☑ LESSON 2 Check

1. Summarize What is the geologic time scale?

....
....
....
....

Use Figure 2 in the lesson to help you answer Questions 2 and 3.

2. Determine Differences How is Precambrian Time different from the other divisions of the geologic time scale?

....
....
....

3. CCC Scale, Proportion, and Quantity How is the geologic time scale divided?

....
....
....
....

4. CCC Stability and Change Explain why you think the geologic time scale will or will not change over the next 20 years.

....
....
....
....
....
....
....

5. SEP Construct Explanations Give an example of physical evidence used to organize Earth's history on the geologic time scale.

....
....
....
....
....
....

Quest CHECK-IN

In this lesson, you learned about the purpose of the geologic time scale and how the segments of the geologic time scale are defined.

SEP Evaluate Evidence How could you organize the fossils of potential dig sites using the geologic time scale?

....
....
....
....

INTERACTIVITY

A Matter of Time

Go online to learn about fossils found at each potential dig site and plot them on the geologic time scale.

uEngineer It! | Defining the Problem | STEM

MS-ESS1-4

Tiny Fossil,
BIG ACCURACY

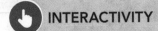

INTERACTIVITY

Determine which absolute dating method will return the most accurate result.

How can you determine the age of a small geologic sample with the greatest precision? You engineer it! An accelerator mass spectrometer is designed for accurate dating with less material.

The Challenge: To develop ways to determine more precisely the absolute age of a geologic event using smaller samples.

Phenomenon Representing a technological leap in absolute dating methods, the accelerator mass spectrometer (AMS) is one of the most important tools scientists use when dating events in Earth's past. Whereas traditional radioactive dating methods might require a 100-gram sample of material, an AMS can help to determine the absolute ages of samples with as little as 20 milligrams. These sensitive devices are also more accurate and can return results in less time than traditional radioactive dating methods. These improvements help geologists organize events in the geologic time scale more accurately and faster. The AMS is particularly helpful when dating more recent events of the Quaternary period, from which only small samples of organic remains may be available for carbon-14 dating.

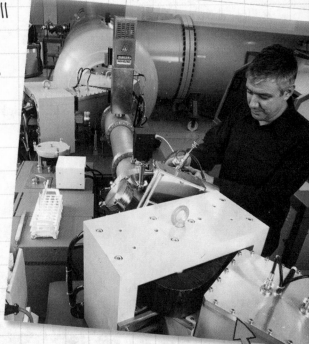

The accelerator mass spectrometer helps scientists to refine the geologic time scale.

DESIGN CHALLENGE Can you make a model of the geologic time scale? Go to the Engineering Design Notebook to find out!

Major Events in Earth's History

Guiding Questions
- How did Earth change in the Paleozoic era?
- How did Earth change in the Mesozoic era?
- How did Earth change in the Cenozoic era?

Connections

Literacy Cite Textual Evidence

Math Represent Quantitative Relationships

MS-ESS1-4

HANDS-ON LAB

uInvestigate Analyze changes in biodiversity over time.

Vocabulary
invertebrate
vertebrate
amphibian
reptile
mass extinction
mammal

Academic Vocabulary
factors
hypothesize

Connect It!

✎ Circle any organisms you recognize in this Carboniferous swamp.

CCC Patterns How was life during the Carboniferous period similar to life today?

....

....

SEP Engaging in Argument from Evidence What do you think conditions were like in this Carboniferous period dragonfly's habitat?

....

....

....

Major Events in the Paleozoic Era

HANDS-ON LAB

Investigate Analyze changes in biodiversity over time.

Earth has a long history of change, starting 4.6 billion years ago when the planet formed. The geologic time scale, interpreted from the rock and fossil records, provides a way to organize that long history of change. The development and evolution of organisms is just one example of the changes that have taken place. For example, **Figure 1** shows how different life was on Earth 300 million years ago.

Through most of Earth's history, during Precambrian time, the only living things were single-celled organisms. Near the end of the Precambrian, more complex living things evolved. Feathery, plantlike organisms anchored themselves to the seafloor. Jellyfish-like organisms floated in the oceans. Then, a much greater variety of living things evolved during the next phase of geologic time—the Paleozoic era.

The Cambrian Explosion During the first part of the Paleozoic era, known as the Cambrian period, life took a big leap forward. Many different kinds of organisms evolved, including some that had hard parts such as shells and outer skeletons. This evolutionary event is called the Cambrian explosion because so many new life forms appeared within a relatively short time. To date these changes, scientists use the law of superposition and other methods to find relative ages and radioactive dating to find absolute ages in the geologic record.

At this time, all animals lived in the sea. Many were animals without backbones, or **invertebrates**. Common invertebrates included jellyfish, worms, sponges, clam-like brachiopods, and trilobites.

Ancient Swamp Life
Figure 1 This artist's drawing shows life in a swampy forest during the Carboniferous period, which occurred about 200 million years after the Cambrian period.

Early Organisms

Figure 2 ✏️ These fossils provide evidence of the evolution of organisms during the Paleozoic era. Write the period during which the organism appeared in the fossil record.

Jawless Fish ....

First Vertebrates and Land Plants The Ordovician period is the second segment of the Paleozoic era. The first vertebrates, including jawless fish, evolved during the Ordovician. A **vertebrate** is an animal with a backbone. The first insects may have evolved at this time, along with land plants.

Plants grew abundantly during the next period, the Silurian. These simple plants grew low to the ground in damp areas. By the Devonian period that followed, plants evolved that could grow in drier areas. Among these plants were the earliest ferns.

Both invertebrates and vertebrates lived in the Devonian seas. Even though the invertebrates were more numerous, the Devonian is often called the Age of Fish. Every main group of fish, including sharks, was present in the oceans. Most fish had jaws, bony skeletons, and scales on their bodies.

Animals Reach Land The Devonian period was also when vertebrates began to live on land. The first land vertebrates were lungfish with strong, muscular fins. The first amphibians evolved from these lungfish. An **amphibian** (am FIB ee un) is an animal that lives part of its life on land and part of its life in water.

Literacy Connection

Cite Textual Evidence
Underline the evidence that supports the statement "Animals and plants evolved further during the Carboniferous Period."

Animals and Plants Evolve Further The Carboniferous period followed the Devonian in the late Paleozoic era. During this period, the amniote egg (an egg filled with special fluids) evolved. This important adaptation allowed animals to lay eggs on land without the eggs drying out. This adaptation coincides with the appearance of reptiles in the fossil record. **Reptiles** have scaly skin and lay eggs that have tough, leathery shells.

During the Carboniferous, winged insects evolved into many new forms, including huge dragonflies and cockroaches. Giant ferns, mosses, and cone-bearing plants formed vast swampy forests. These plants resembled plants that live in tropical and temperate areas today.

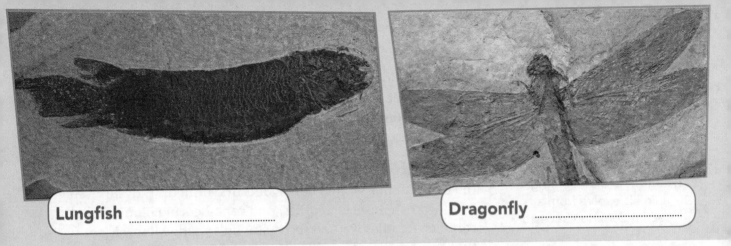

Lungfish ....

Dragonfly ....

Pangaea Over the course of the Paleozoic era, Earth's continents slowly moved together to form a great landmass, or supercontinent, called Pangaea (pan JEE uh). The formation of Pangaea caused deserts to expand in the tropics and sheets of ice to cover land closer to the South Pole.

Mass Extinction The organisms in **Figure 2** represent the huge diversity of life that evolved during the Paleozoic era. However, during the Permian period at the end of the Paleozoic, a major change occurred and most species of life on Earth died out during the worst extinction event in Earth's history. This was a **mass extinction**, an event during which many types of living things became extinct at the same time. Scientists estimate that about 90 percent of all ocean species and 70 percent of species on land died out. Even widespread organisms such as trilobites became extinct.

Scientists aren't sure what caused this extinction. Some scientists think multiple volcanoes erupted so much dust and debris that the energy from the sun was blocked. This would have prevented plants from performing photosynthesis. Other scientists think a rise in global temperatures was to blame. Scientists have also found that the amount of carbon dioxide in the oceans increased and the amount of oxygen declined. It would have been difficult for organisms to quickly adjust to these changes. All of these **factors** likely contributed to the mass extinction.

✓READING CHECK **Cite Textual Evidence** According to the text, what impact did the amniote egg have on lifeforms on Earth?

....

....

....

....

....

👆 **INTERACTIVITY**

Observe fossils to make deductions about the organisms and their environments.

Academic Vocabulary
What two factors determined what you did over the weekend?

....

....

....

....

....

....

Mesozoic Winged Animals

Figure 3 This illustration shows an artist's idea of what a *Dimorphodon* (a type of pterosaur) and an *Archaeopteryx* looked like.

1. **Claim** Did these winged animals evolve from a recent common ancestor?

....

2. **Evidence** List the evidence that supports your claim

....

....

....

....

....

3. **Reasoning** Explain how your evidence supports your claim.

....

....

....

....

....

....

....

Major Events in the Mesozoic Era

Mass extinctions are followed by increases in evolution and variation. The mass extinction at the end of the Paleozoic era became an opportunity for many new life forms, including dinosaurs, to develop in the Mesozoic era.

Age of Reptiles Some living things managed to survive the Permian mass extinction. Plants and animals that survived included fish, insects, reptiles, and cone-bearing plants called conifers. Reptiles were so successful during the Mesozoic era that this time is often called the Age of Reptiles. The first dinosaurs appeared during the first period of the Mesozoic era, called the Triassic period.

First Mammals Mammals also first appeared during the Triassic period. A **mammal** is a vertebrate that controls its own body temperature and feeds milk to its young. Mammals in the Triassic period were very small—about the size of a mouse.

Reptiles and Birds During the Jurassic period, the second segment of the Mesozoic era, dinosaurs were the dominant land animals. Scientists have identified several hundred different kinds of dinosaurs, including some that ate plants and some that were predators. One plant-eating dinosaur, *Brachiosaurus*, was 26 meters long!

The ocean and seas during this period were also filled with diverse life forms, including sharks, rays, giant marine crocodiles, and plesiosaurs. Plesiosaurs had long necks and paddle-like fins.

Late in the Jurassic, the first known birds appeared in the skies. *Archaeopteryx*, which means "ancient winged one," is thought to have evolved from a dinosaur. The sky also had flying reptiles, called pterosaurs, and many varieties of insects. Use **Figure 3** to compare *Archaeopteryx* and a type of pterosaur called *Dimorphodon*.

Dimorphodon

Archaeopteryx

Flowering Plants The Cretaceous period is the final and longest segment of the Mesozoic era. Reptiles, including dinosaurs, were still widespread throughout the Cretaceous. Ancient birds evolved better adaptations for flying and began to replace flying reptiles.

One of the most important events of the Cretaceous period was the evolution of flowering plants, or angiosperms. Unlike conifers, flowering plants produce seeds that are inside a fruit. Many flowering plants you may recognize today first appeared during this time, such as magnolias, figs, and willows.

Another Mass Extinction

At the end of the Cretaceous, another mass extinction occurred. Scientists **hypothesize** that this mass extinction occurred when an asteroid struck Earth at a time when extreme volcanic activity in the area that is now India had weakened environments. This mass extinction wiped out more than half of all plant and animal groups, including the dinosaurs. Use **Figure 4** to illustrate the event.

✓ READING CHECK **Use Information** How did organisms from the Mesozoic era differ from organisms of the Paleozoic?

....

....

....

👆 INTERACTIVITY

Examine evidence that shows major changes over time.

Reflect Which major event or time in Earth's history would you most like to witness? In your science notebook, describe the event or time period and why you would like to experience it.

Academic Vocabulary

Use *hypothesize* in a sentence about a subject other than science.

....

....

....

Model It !

The End of the Dinosaurs

Figure 4 Scientists hypothesize that an asteroid hit Earth near present-day southeastern Mexico. Show how this event, combined with the environment at the time, contributed to the mass extinction.

SEP Develop Models ✏ Complete the comic strip. Draw events that led to the extinction of the dinosaurs. Label each stage. Add a title.

Title: ....

Math Toolbox

Comparing Mammal Height

Many giant mammals evolved in the Cenozoic era. The *Megatherium* is related to the modern sloth but is much taller.

1. **Measure** Use the ruler to measure the height of each sloth.

   Megatherium height: about ....

   Modern sloth height: about ....

2. **Represent Quantitative Relationships** About how many times taller was *Megatherium* than a modern sloth? Complete the equation below, in which *m* is the height of *Megatherium* and *s* is the height of the modern sloth.

   $m = s \times$ ....

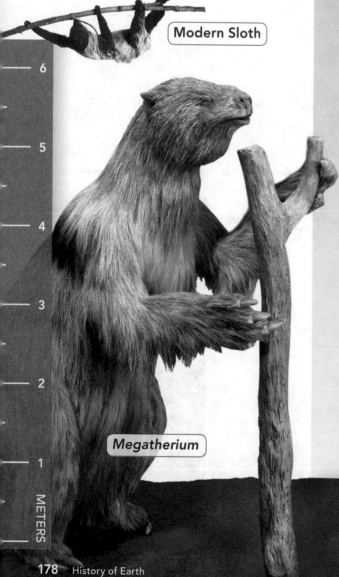

Modern Sloth

Megatherium

METERS

Major Events in the Cenozoic Era

During the Mesozoic era, small mammals had to compete with dinosaurs and other animals for food and places to live. The mass extinction at the end of that era created an opportunity for the species that did survive, including some mammals. During the Cenozoic era that followed, mammals evolved to live in many different environments—on land, in water, and even in the air. Geologists have found evidence for the spread of mammals in the fossils, rocks, and sediment of the early Cenozoic era.

Mammals Thrive The Cenozoic begins with the Paleogene and Neogene periods. During these periods, Earth's climate became gradually cooler over time. As the continents drifted apart, ocean basins widened and mammals such as whales and dolphins evolved. On land, mammals flourished. Some birds and mammals became very large. Forests thinned, making space for flowering plants and grasses to become more dominant.

Ice Ages At the start of the Quaternary period, large sheets of ice began to appear on Earth's surface. Earth's climate continued to cool and warm in cycles, causing a series of ice ages followed by warmer periods. During an ice age, about 30 percent of Earth's surface was covered in thick glaciers. The latest warm period began between 10,000 and 20,000 years ago. During that time, sea levels rose and most of the glaciers melted.

Humans The Quaternary period is sometimes referred to as the "Age of Humans." *Homo erectus*, an ancestor of modern humans, appears in the fossil record near the start of the period, while modern humans appeared about 190,000 years ago. By about 12,000 to 15,000 years ago, humans had migrated to every continent except Antarctica.

How Scientists Organize Earth's History

Figure 5 This timeline shows major events in Earth's history. It is a model that you can use to study events that occur over geologic time. (Note that, to make the timeline easier to read, periods are not drawn to scale.) Circle the periods during which mass extinctions occurred.

Events	Period	Began (Millions of Years Ago)	
Earth forms. First single-celled and multi-celled organisms evolve.		4,600	PRECAMBRIAN TIME
"Explosion" of new forms of life occurs. Invertebrates such as trilobites are common.	Cambrian	541	PALEOZOIC ERA
First vertebrates, insects, and land plants evolve.	Ordovician	485	
Early fish are common in seas.	Silurian	444	
"Age of Fish" occurs, with many different kinds of fish. Lungfish and amphibians first reach land.	Devonian	419	
Appalachian Mountains form. Reptiles and giant insects evolve. Ferns and cone-bearing plants form forests.	Carboniferous	359	
Pangaea forms. Mass extinction kills most species.	Permian	299	
Reptiles flourish, including the first dinosaurs. First mammals evolve.	Triassic	252	MESOZOIC ERA
Dinosaurs become common. First birds evolve.	Jurassic	201	
Dinosaurs are widespread. Birds begin to replace flying reptiles. Flowering plants appear. Mass extinction occurs.	Cretaceous	145	
Mammals flourish. Grasses first spread widely.	Paleogene	66	CENOZOIC ERA
The Andes and Himalayas form. Some mammals and birds become very large.	Neogene	23	
Ice ages occur. Many kinds of animals thrive. First modern humans evolve.	Quarternary	2.6	

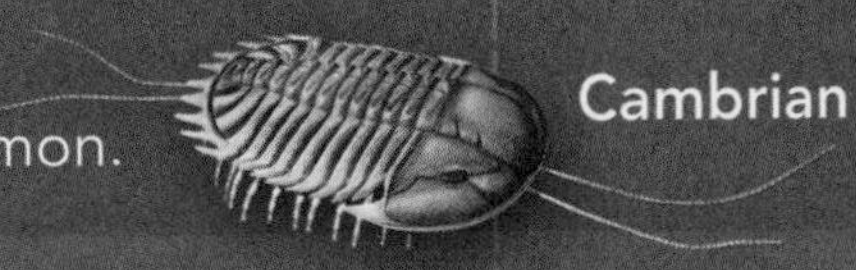

MS-ESS1-4

1. **Identify** During which era was the "Age of Reptiles"?

....

2. **Sequence** Arrange the following organisms in order from earliest to latest appearance: amphibians, jawless fish, trilobites, bony fish.

....

....

3. **CCC Cause and Effect** Name two possible causes of the mass extinction at the end of the Paleozoic.

....

....

4. **SEP Construct Explanations** What factors allowed new organisms to evolve and thrive during the Cenozoic era?

....

....

....

....

....

5. **Synthesize Information** Why do you think scientists use mass extinctions to separate one era from another?

....

....

....

....

....

....

....

....

6. **SEP Cite Evidence** Identify a major event in Earth's past and describe the supporting evidence for that event you would expect to observe in the fossil record.

....

....

....

....

....

Quest CHECK-IN

In this lesson, you learned about major events that help to define and organize Earth's history.

Evaluate Reasoning How can knowing about Earth's history help you to choose your dig site?

....

....

....

....

👆 **INTERACTIVITY**

Time to Choose the Dig Site

Go online to conduct research about *Dimetrodon* to make the final site selection.

Global to Local

MS-ESS1-4

A New Mass Extinction?

When a species dies out, we say it is extinct. When large numbers of species die out at the same time, scientists use the term *mass extinction*. Scientists know of multiple mass extinctions in Earth's history. Some suggest that another mass extinction is approaching.

One factor that can lead to extinctions is the introduction of plant and animal species into new environments. Some of this is due to species migration. Animals and plants can move into new areas where temperature and climate patterns have become more favorable due to global warming. However, most species are brought to new areas by humans. In many cases, this leads to the disappearance of native species.

Habitat loss is another factor that leads to extinctions. When habitats are lost, the species that live within them no longer have the space or resources to live. As the human population increases, so has the human need for resources, such as fuel, land, and food. Habitats are cleared or changed to meet those needs, and the organisms that lived there may die off. For example, burning and clearing tropical forests threatens many endangered primates.

Climate change caused by global warming may also lead to extinctions. Our increased use of fossil fuels and the accompanying rise in carbon dioxide in the atmosphere has led to a steady increase in global temperatures. As temperatures rise, environments change. Species that cannot adapt to the changes may die out.

Most scientists agree that there is a real threat of another mass extinction. However, there are still steps people can take to prevent or minimize the loss of our biodiversity.

Urban development to accommodate a growing human population leads to habitat loss.

MY COMMUNITY

What steps can you take in your community to change our path away from mass extinction? Use the library and the Internet to find facts and evidence that will support your ideas.

☑TOPIC 4 Review and Assess

1 Determining Ages of Rocks

MS-ESS1-4

1. Which term describes a gap in the geologic record that occurs when sedimentary rocks cover an eroded surface?
   A. extrusion   B. fault
   C. intrusion   D. unconformity

2. Which term describes the time it takes for half of a radioactive element's atoms to decay?
   A. absolute age   B. half-life
   C. radioactive decay   D. relative age

3. Which statement **best** describes one rule for determining the relative age of a rock layer?
   A. A fault is always younger than the rock it cuts through.
   B. An extrusion is always older than the rocks below it.
   C. An index fossil is always younger than the rock layer it occurs in.
   D. An intrusion is always older than the rock layers around it.

4. Which of the following conclusions can geologists draw about a limestone rock layer based on the law of superposition?
   A. The limestone layer is 2 million years old.
   B. The limestone layer contains 2 million fossils.
   C. The limestone layer is younger than the sandstone layer below it.
   D. The limestone layer is the same age as another layer 100 hundred kilometers away.

5. A geologist finds an area of undisturbed sedimentary rock. The .... layer is most likely the oldest.

6. Radioactive dating is a method used by geologists to determine the .... age of rocks.

7. **SEP Construct Explanations** A geologist finds identical index fossils in a rock layer in the Grand Canyon in Arizona and in a rock layer 675 kilometers away in Utah. What can she infer about the ages of the two rock layers?

....

....

....

8. **Sequence** Using the numbers and letters, list the rock layers and formations in the diagram in order from oldest to youngest. Cite evidence from the diagram to explain your answer.

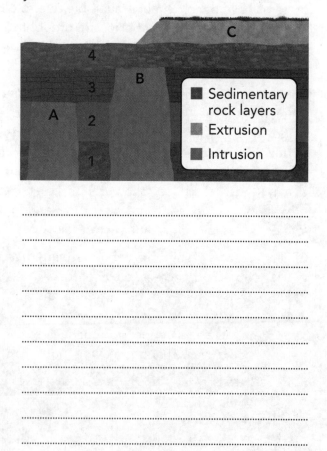

■ Sedimentary rock layers
■ Extrusion
■ Intrusion

....

....

....

....

....

....

....

....

....

....

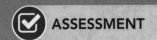
2 Geologic Time Scale

MS-ESS1-4

9. Into which units is the geologic time scale subdivided?
  A. relative ages   **B.** absolute ages
  C. months and days   **D.** eras and periods

10. What do geologists **mostly** study to develop the geologic time scale?
  A. Earth's rotation
  B. tectonic plate motions
  C. volcanoes and earthquakes
  D. rock layers and index fossils

11. How do geologists use radioactive dating in developing the geologic time scale?
  A. to identify index fossils
  B. to identify types of rocks
  C. to place rocks in order by relative age
  D. to determine the absolute age of rocks

12. The geologic time scale is a record of
  .... and ....

13. SEP Construct Explanations Why do geologists need the geologic time scale? Give two reasons.

  ....
  ....
  ....
  ....
  ....
  ....
  ....
  ....

3 Major Events in Earth's History

MS-ESS1-4

14. Which event occurred in the Cenozoic era?
  A. first mammals
  B. spread of mammals
  C. first flowering plants
  D. spread of ferns and conifers

15. What were Earth's earliest multicellular organisms?
  A. bacteria   **B.** land plants
  C. vertebrates   **D.** invertebrates

16. The first birds evolved during the
  .... era.

17. SEP Develop Models Draw what the Devonian period of the Paleozoic era might have looked like. Think about the events that define the Devonian period when making your model.

MS-ESS1-4

Evidence-Based Assessment

A team of geologists explores an area of land that was once an ancient sea. They dig for fossils of marine organisms at three locations. The geologists collect and record information about the fossils they have discovered and the rock layers that the fossils were found in. The data are summarized in the diagram.

The geologists attempt to identify an index fossil to help them analyze the relative ages of the rock layers and to determine how the layers at the three sites correspond to each other. The researchers attempt to determine the relative ages of the layers and the marine organisms whose fossils they have dug up.

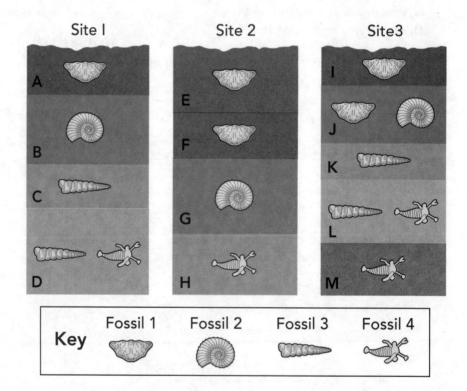

1. **SEP Interpret Data** Which of the following is an index fossil?
   A. Fossil 1   C. Fossil 3
   B. Fossil 2   D. Fossil 4

2. **Evaluate Quantity** Which statements about the relative ages of the rock layers is true? Select all that apply.
   ☐ Layers B, G, and J are the same age.
   ☐ Layer E is the youngest layer.
   ☐ Layers D, H, and J are the same age.
   ☐ Layer M is the oldest layer.
   ☐ Layer A is the youngest layer.
   ☐ Layers D and H are the oldest layers.

3. **Apply Scientific Reasoning** Based on the data, what can you conclude about the relative ages of Fossils 1 and 2? What scientific law can you use to support your response?

   ....
   ....
   ....
   ....
   ....
   ....
   ....
   ....
   ....

4. **SEP Engage in Argument** A peer claims that Fossil 2 is older than Fossil 3. Using evidence from the rock layers, explain why the evidence does not support their claim.

   ....
   ....
   ....
   ....
   ....
   ....
   ....
   ....

5. **SEP Construct Explanations** Fossil 2 is about 300 million years old. Testing reveals that Layer M is about 400 million years old. The geologists conclude that Fossil 3 is an organism that likely lived about 350 million years ago. Do you agree? Support your answer using evidence from the diagram.

   ....
   ....
   ....
   ....
   ....
   ....
   ....

Quest FINDINGS

Complete the Quest!

Phenomenon Present your choice of dig site in a report to the head of the science museum that is sponsoring the *Dimetrodon* exhibit. In your report, include evidence and scientific reasoning that supports your choice.

Evaluate Your Plan What roles did the rock and fossil record play in determining your choice of dig site?

....
....
....
....

INTERACTIVITY

Reflect on the Big Fossil Hunt

185

MS-ESS1-4

Core Sampling Through Time

How can you **determine** the **relative ages of rock layers** in different locations?

Background

Phenomenon Visitors to a local state park see a variety of rocks and fossils on the surface in different locations. They often ask: Are the rocks here the same age as those over there? In your role as volunteer park ranger, how will you answer? You will need to find out how the ages of the rocks throughout the park compare.

You know that you can learn about the order of events in Earth's history by studying rocks. However, geologists cannot simply flip through layers of sedimentary rock like the pages in a magazine to study them. Instead, they must analyze samples taken from deep below the surface. In a process called coring, hollow tubes are driven into sedimentary rock layers. When the tubes are pulled out, they contain samples of each layer.

In this activity, you will illustrate the geologic history of the park using the data you gather through core sampling.

Materials

(per group)

- four models positioned around the classroom representing rock layers
- plastic gloves
- metric ruler
- large-diameter drinking straw
- long dowel or rod that fits into the straw
- several sheets of paper
- colored pencils

Safety

Be sure to follow all safety guidelines provided by your teacher. The Safety Appendix of your textbook provides more details about the safety icons.

Plan Your Investigation

1. Your teacher positioned four models around the classroom. The models represent sedimentary rock layers, some with index fossils, in different locations throughout the park.

2. Design an investigation to discover the geologic history of the park by drilling and analyzing core samples. Think about the following questions as you form your plan:

- In which locations should you drill to get a complete picture of the rocks throughout the park so you can compare their ages?

- How many core samples will you drill in each location?

- How will you record what you observe in the core samples?

- How will you compare the locations of sediment layers and index fossils?

- How will you present your findings?

3. Use the space provided to summarize your investigation. Show your plan to your teacher for approval.

4. Conduct your investigation, record your observations, and report your findings according to your plan.

иDemonstrate Go online for a downloadable worksheet of this lab.

Procedure

....
....
....
....
....
....
....
....
....
....
....
....

Evidence Gathered from Core Samples

Analyze and Interpret Data

1. **SEP Develop Models** Use your observations and analysis to make a diagram of the complete geologic history of the park.

2. **SEP Use Models** Compare the geologic record at the different locations represented by your model core samples. Explain any differences you observe.

....

....

3. **CCC Patterns** Which rock layers at the different locations do you think are the same age? Explain your answer using evidence.

....

....

4. **Apply Scientific Reasoning** Choose two core samples that represent different locations in the park. Compare the ages of the rocks on the surface. Explain how you determined their relative ages.

....

....

....

....

....

SEP.1, SEP.8

The Meaning of Science

Science Skills

Reflect Think about a time you misplaced something and could not find it. Write a sentence defining the problem. What science skills could you use to solve the problem? Explain how you would use at least three of the skills in the table.

Science is a way of learning about the natural world. It involves asking questions, making predictions, and collecting information to see if the answer is right or wrong.

The table lists some of the skills that scientists use. You use some of these skills every day. For example, you may observe and evaluate your lunch options before choosing what to eat.

Skill	Definition
classifying	grouping together items that are alike or that have shared characteristics
evaluating	comparing observations and data to reach a conclusion
inferring	explaining or interpreting observations
investigating	studying or researching a subject to discover facts or to reveal new information
making models	creating representations of complex objects or processes
observing	using one or more of your senses to gather information
predicting	making a statement or claim about what will happen based on past experience or evidence

Scientific Attitudes

Curiosity often drives scientists to learn about the world around them. Creativity is useful for coming up with inventive ways to solve problems. Such qualities and attitudes, and the ability to keep an open mind, are essential for scientists.

When sharing results or findings, honesty and ethics are also essential. Ethics refers to rules for knowing right from wrong.

Being skeptical is also important. This means having doubts about things based on past experiences and evidence. Skepticism helps to prevent accepting data and results that may not be true.

Scientists must also avoid bias—likes or dislikes of people, ideas, or things. They must avoid experimental bias, which is a mistake that may make an experiment's preferred outcome more likely.

Scientific Reasoning

Scientific reasoning depends on being logical and objective. When you are objective, you use evidence and apply logic to draw conclusions. Being subjective means basing conclusions on personal feelings, biases, or opinions. Subjective reasoning can interfere with science and skew results. Objective reasoning helps scientists use observations to reach conclusions about the natural world.

Scientists use two types of objective reasoning: deductive and inductive. Deductive reasoning involves starting with a general idea or theory and applying it to a situation. For example, the theory of plate tectonics indicates that earthquakes happen mostly where tectonic plates meet. You could then draw the conclusion, or deduce, that California has many earthquakes because tectonic plates meet there.

In inductive reasoning, you make a generalization from a specific observation. When scientists collect data in an experiment and draw a conclusion based on that data, they use inductive reasoning. For example, if fertilizer causes one set of plants to grow faster than another, you might infer that the fertilizer promotes plant growth.

Make Meaning
Think about a bias the marine biologist in the photo could show that results in paying more or less attention to one kind of organism over others. Make a prediction about how that bias could affect the biologist's survey of the coral reef.

Write About It
Suppose it is raining when you go to sleep one night. When you wake up the next morning, you observe frozen puddles on the ground and icicles on tree branches. Use scientific reasoning to draw a conclusion about the air temperature outside. Support your conclusion using deductive or inductive reasoning.

191

SEP.1, SEP.2, SEP.3, SEP.4, CCC.4

Science Processes

Scientific Inquiry

Scientists contribute to scientific knowledge by conducting investigations and drawing conclusions. The process often begins with an observation that leads to a question, which is then followed by the development of a hypothesis. This is known as scientific inquiry.

One of the first steps in scientific inquiry is asking questions. However, it's important to make a question specific with a narrow focus so the investigation will not be too broad. A biologist may want to know all there is to know about wolves, for example. But a good, focused question for a specific inquiry might be "How many offspring does the average female wolf produce in her lifetime?"

A hypothesis is a possible answer to a scientific question. A hypothesis must be testable. For something to be testable, researchers must be able to carry out an investigation and gather evidence that will either support or disprove the hypothesis.

Scientific Models

Models are tools that scientists use to study phenomena indirectly. A model is any representation of an object or process. Illustrations, dioramas, globes, diagrams, computer programs, and mathematical equations are all examples of scientific models. For example, a diagram of Earth's crust and mantle can help you to picture layers deep below the surface and understand events such as volcanic eruptions.

Models also allow scientists to represent objects that are either very large, such as our solar system, or very small, such as a molecule of DNA. Models can also represent processes that occur over a long period of time, such as the changes that have occurred throughout Earth's history.

Models are helpful, but they have limitations. Physical models are not made of the same materials as the objects they represent. Most models of complex objects or processes show only major parts, stages, or relationships. Many details are left out. Therefore, you may not be able to learn as much from models as you would through direct observation.

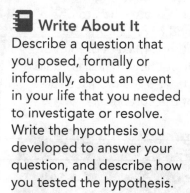

Write About It Describe a question that you posed, formally or informally, about an event in your life that you needed to investigate or resolve. Write the hypothesis you developed to answer your question, and describe how you tested the hypothesis.

Reflect Identify the benefits and limitations of using a plastic model of DNA, as shown here.

Science Experiments

An experiment or investigation must be well planned to produce valid results. In planning an experiment, you must identify the independent and dependent variables. You must also do as much as possible to remove the effects of other variables. A controlled experiment is one in which you test only one variable at a time.

For example, suppose you plan a controlled experiment to learn how the type of material affects the speed at which sound waves travel through it. The only variable that should change is the type of material. This way, if the speed of sound changes, you know that it is a result of a change in the material, not another variable such as the thickness of the material or the type of sound used.

You should also remove bias from any investigation. You may inadvertently introduce bias by selecting subjects you like and avoiding those you don't like. Scientists often conduct investigations by taking random samples to avoid ending up with biased results.

Once you plan your investigation and begin to collect data, it's important to record and organize the data. You may wish to use a graph to display and help you to interpret the data.

Communicating is the sharing of ideas and results with others through writing and speaking. Communicating data and conclusions is a central part of science.

Scientists share knowledge, including new findings, theories, and techniques for collecting data. Conferences, journals, and websites help scientists to communicate with each other. Popular media, including newspapers, magazines, and social media sites, help scientists to share their knowledge with nonscientists. However, before the results of investigations are shared and published, other scientists should review the experiment for possible sources of error, such as bias and unsupported conclusions.

Write About It

List four ways you could communicate the results of a scientific study about the health of sea turtles in the Pacific Ocean.

SEP.1, SEP.6, SEP.7, SEP.8

Scientific Knowledge

Scientific Explanations

Suppose you learn that adult flamingos are pink because of the food they eat. This statement is a scientific explanation—it describes how something in nature works or explains why it happens. Scientists from different fields use methods such as researching information, designing experiments, and making models to form scientific explanations. Scientific explanations often result from many years of work and multiple investigations conducted by many scientists.

Scientific Theories and Laws

A scientific law is a statement that describes what you can expect to occur every time under a particular set of conditions. A scientific law describes an observed pattern in nature, but it does not attempt to explain it. For example, the law of superposition describes what you can expect to find in terms of the ages of layers of rock. Geologists use this observed pattern to determine the relative ages of sedimentary rock layers. But the law does not explain why the pattern occurs.

By contrast, a scientific theory is a well-tested explanation for a wide range of observations or experimental results. It provides details and describes causes of observed patterns. Something is elevated to a theory only when there is a large body of evidence that supports it. However, a scientific theory can be changed or overturned when new evidence is found.

Write About It
Choose two fields of science that interest you. Describe a method used to develop scientific explanations in each field.

SEP Construct Explanations Complete the table to compare and contrast a scientific theory and a scientific law.

	Scientific Theory	Scientific Law
Definition		
Does it attempt to explain a pattern observed in nature?		

Analyzing Scientific Explanations

To analyze scientific explanations that you hear on the news or read in a book such as this one, you need scientific literacy. Scientific literacy means understanding scientific terms and principles well enough to ask questions, evaluate information, and make decisions. Scientific reasoning gives you a process to apply. This includes looking for bias and errors in the research, evaluating data, and identifying faulty reasoning. For example, by evaluating how a survey was conducted, you may find a serious flaw in the researchers' methods.

Evidence and Opinions

The basis for scientific explanations is empirical evidence. Empirical evidence includes the data and observations that have been collected through scientific processes. Satellite images, photos, and maps of mountains and volcanoes are all examples of empirical evidence that support a scientific explanation about Earth's tectonic plates. Scientists look for patterns when they analyze this evidence. For example, they might see a pattern that mountains and volcanoes often occur near tectonic plate boundaries.

To evaluate scientific information, you must first distinguish between evidence and opinion. In science, evidence includes objective observations and conclusions that have been repeated. Evidence may or may not support a scientific claim. An opinion is a subjective idea that is formed from evidence, but it cannot be confirmed by evidence.

Write About It

Suppose the conservation committee of a town wants to gauge residents' opinions about a proposal to stock the local ponds with fish every spring. The committee pays for a survey to appear on a web site that is popular with people who like to fish. The results of the survey show 78 people in favor of the proposal and two against it. Do you think the survey's results are valid? Explain.

Make Meaning

Explain what empirical evidence the photograph reveals.

SEP.3, SEP.4

Tools of Science

Measurement

Making measurements using standard units is important in all fields of science. This allows scientists to repeat and reproduce other experiments, as well as to understand the precise meaning of the results of others. Scientists use a measurement system called the International System of Units, or SI.

For each type of measurement, there is a series of units that are greater or less than each other. The unit a scientist uses depends on what is being measured. For example, a geophysicist tracking the movements of tectonic plates may use centimeters, as plates tend to move small amounts each year. Meanwhile, a marine biologist might measure the movement of migrating bluefin tuna on the scale of kilometers.

Units for length, mass, volume, and density are based on powers of ten—a meter is equal to 100 centimeters or 1000 millimeters. Units of time do not follow that pattern. There are 60 seconds in a minute, 60 minutes in an hour, and 24 hours in a day. These units are based on patterns that humans perceived in nature. Units of temperature are based on scales that are set according to observations of nature. For example, 0°C is the temperature at which pure water freezes, and 100°C is the temperature at which it boils.

Write About It

Suppose you are planning an investigation in which you must measure the dimensions of several small mineral samples that fit in your hand. Which metric unit or units will you most likely use? Explain your answer.

Measurement	Metric units
Length or distance	meter (m), kilometer (km), centimeter (cm), millimeter (mm) 1 km = 1,000 m 1 cm = 10 mm 1 m = 100 cm
Mass	kilogram (kg), gram (g), milligram (mg) 1 kg = 1,000 g 1 g = 1,000 mg
Volume	cubic meter (m³), cubic centimeter (cm³) 1 m³ = 1,000,000 cm³
Density	kilogram per cubic meter (kg/m³), gram per cubic centimeter (g/cm³) 1,000 kg/m³ = 1 g/cm³
Temperature	degrees Celsius (°C), kelvin (K) 1°C = 273 K
Time	hour (h), minute (m), second (s)

Math Skills

Using numbers to collect and interpret data involves math skills that are essential in science. For example, you use math skills when you estimate the number of birds in an entire forest after counting the actual number of birds in ten trees.

Scientists evaluate measurements and estimates for their precision and accuracy. In science, an accurate measurement is very close to the actual value. Precise measurements are very close, or nearly equal, to each other. Reliable measurements are both accurate and precise. An imprecise value may be a sign of an error in data collection. This kind of anomalous data may be excluded to avoid skewing the data and harming the investigation.

Other math skills include performing specific calculations, such as finding the mean, or average, value in a data set. The mean can be calculated by adding up all of the values in the data set and then dividing that sum by the number of values.

Hour	Number of Ducks Observed at a Pond
1	12
2	10
3	2
4	14
5	13
6	10
7	11

SEP Use Mathematics The data table shows how many ducks were seen at a pond every hour over the course of seven hours. Is there a data point that seems anomalous? If so, cross out that data point. Then, calculate the mean number of ducks on the pond. Round the mean to the nearest whole number.

Graphs

Graphs help scientists to interpret data by helping them to find trends or patterns in the data. A line graph displays data that show how one variable (the dependent or outcome variable) changes in response to another (the independent or test variable). The slope and shape of a graph line can reveal patterns and help scientists to make predictions. For example, line graphs can help you to spot patterns of change over time.

Scientists use bar graphs to compare data across categories or subjects that may not affect each other. The heights of the bars make it easy to compare those quantities. A circle graph, also known as a pie chart, shows the proportions of different parts of a whole.

📓 **Write About It**
You and a friend record the distance you travel every 15 minutes on a one-hour bike trip. Your friend wants to display the data as a circle graph. Explain whether or not this is the best type of graph to display your data. If not, suggest another graph to use.

SEP.1, SEP.2, SEP.3, SEP.6

The Engineering Design Process

Engineers are builders and problem solvers. Chemical engineers experiment with new fuels made from algae. Civil engineers design roadways and bridges. Bioengineers develop medical devices and prosthetics. The common trait among engineers is an ability to identify problems and design solutions to solve them. Engineers use a creative process that relies on scientific methods to help guide them from a concept or idea all the way to the final product.

Define the Problem

To identify or define a problem, different questions need to be asked: *What are the effects of the problem? What are the likely causes? What other factors could be involved?* Sometimes the obvious, immediate cause of a problem may be the result of another problem that may not be immediately apparent. For example, climate change results in different weather patterns, which in turn can affect organisms that live in certain habitats. So engineers must be aware of all the possible effects of potential solutions. Engineers must also take into account how well different solutions deal with the different causes of the problem.

Reflect Write about a problem that you encountered in your life that had both immediate, obvious causes as well as less-obvious and less-immediate ones.

ENGINEERING *Design Process*

- **?** DEFINE the problem
- Develop POSSIBLE SOLUTIONS
- DESIGN AND BUILD a solution
- ✓ REDESIGN AND RETEST your solution
- **!** COMMUNICATE your solution
- ✓ TEST AND EVALUATE your solution

As engineers consider problems and design solutions, they must identify and categorize the criteria and constraints of the project.

Criteria are the factors that must be met or accomplished by the solution. For example, a gardener who wants to protect outdoor plants from deer and rabbits may say that the criteria for the solution are "plants are no longer eaten" and "plant growth is not inhibited in any way." The gardener then knows the plants cannot simply be sealed off from the environment, because the plants will not receive sunlight and water.

The same gardener will likely have constraints on his solution, such as budget for materials and time that is available for working on the project. By setting constraints, a solution can be designed that will be successful without introducing a new set of problems. No one wants to spend $500 on materials to protect $100 worth of tomatoes and cucumbers.

Develop Possible Solutions

After the problem has been identified, and the criteria and constraints identified, an engineer will consider possible solutions. This often involves working in teams with other engineers and designers to brainstorm ideas and research materials that can be used in the design.

It's important for engineers to think creatively and explore all potential solutions. If you wanted to design a bicycle that was safer and easier to ride than a traditional bicycle, then you would want more than just one or two solutions. Having multiple ideas to choose from increases the likelihood that you will develop a solution that meets the criteria and constraints. In addition, different ideas that result from brainstorming can often lead to new and better solutions to an existing problem.

Make Meaning
Using the example of a garden that is vulnerable to wild animals such as deer, make a list of likely constraints on an engineering solution to the problem you identified before. Determine if there are common traits among the constraints, and identify categories for them.

Design a Solution

Engineers then develop the idea that they feel best solves the problem. Once a solution has been chosen, engineers and designers get to work building a model or prototype of the solution. A model may involve sketching on paper or using computer software to construct a model of the solution. A prototype is a working model of the solution.

Building a model or prototype helps an engineer determine whether a solution meets the criteria and stays within the constraints. During this stage of the process, engineers must often deal with new problems and make any necessary adjustments to the model or prototype.

Test and Evaluate a Solution

Whether testing a model or a prototype, engineers use scientific processes to evaluate their solutions. Multiple experiments, tests, or trials are conducted, data are evaluated, and results and analyses are communicated. New criteria or constraints may emerge as a result of testing. In most cases, a solution will require some refinement or revision, even if it has been through successful testing. Refining a solution is necessary if there are new constraints, such as less money or available materials. Additional testing may be done to ensure that a solution satisfies local, state, or federal laws or standards.

Make Meaning Think about an aluminum beverage can. What would happen if the price or availability of aluminum changed so much that cans needed to be made of a new material? What would the criteria and constraints be on the development of a new can?

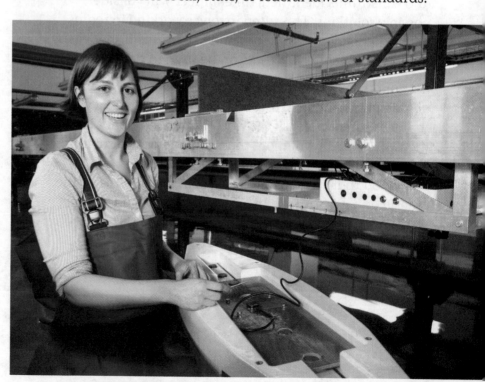

A naval architect sets up a model to test how the the hull's design responds to waves.

Communicate the Solution

Engineers need to communicate the final design to the people who will manufacture the product. This may include sketches, detailed drawings, computer simulations, and written text. Engineers often provide evidence that was collected during the testing stage. This evidence may include graphs and data tables that support the decisions made for the final design.

If there is feedback about the solution, then the engineers and designers must further refine the solution. This might involve making minor adjustments to the design, or it might mean bigger modifications to the design based on new criteria or constraints. Any changes in the design will require additional testing to make sure that the changes work as intended.

Redesign and Retest the Solution

At different steps in the engineering and design process, a solution usually must be revised and retested. Many designs fail to work perfectly, even after models and prototypes are built, tested, and evaluated. Engineers must be ready to analyze new results and deal with any new problems that arise. Troubleshooting, or fixing design problems, allows engineers to adjust the design to improve on how well the solution meets the need.

SEP Communicate Information Suppose you are an engineer at an aerospace company. Your team is designing a rover to be used on a future NASA space mission. A family member doesn't understand why so much of your team's time is taken up with testing and retesting the rover design. What are three things you would tell your relative to explain why testing and retesting are so important to the engineering and design process?

....

....

....

....

....

....

....

....

Safety Symbols

These symbols warn of possible dangers in the laboratory and remind you to work carefully.

 Safety Goggles Wear safety goggles to protect your eyes in any activity involving chemicals, flames or heating, or glassware.

 Lab Apron Wear a laboratory apron to protect your skin and clothing from damage.

 Breakage Handle breakable materials, such as glassware, with care. Do not touch broken glassware.

 Heat-Resistant Gloves Use an oven mitt or other hand protection when handling hot materials, such as hot plates or hot glassware.

 Plastic Gloves Wear disposable plastic gloves when working with harmful chemicals and organisms. Keep your hands away from your face, and dispose of the gloves according to your teacher's instructions.

 Heating Use a clamp or tongs to pick up hot glassware. Do not touch hot objects with your bare hands.

 Flames Before you work with flames, tie back loose hair and clothing. Follow your teacher's instructions about lighting and extinguishing flames.

 No Flames When using flammable materials, make sure there are no flames, sparks, or other exposed heat sources present.

 Corrosive Chemical Avoid getting acid or other corrosive chemicals on your skin or clothing or in your eyes. Do not inhale the vapors. Wash your hands after the activity.

 Poison Do not let any poisonous chemical come into contact with your skin, and do not inhale its vapors. Wash your hands when you are finished with the activity.

 Fumes Work in a well-ventilated area when harmful vapors may be involved. Avoid inhaling vapors directly. Test an odor only when directed to do so by your teacher, and use a wafting motion to direct the vapor toward your nose.

 Sharp Object Scissors, scalpels, knives, needles, pins, and tacks can cut your skin. Always direct a sharp edge or point away from yourself and others.

 Animal Safety Treat live or preserved animals or animal parts with care to avoid harming the animals or yourself. Wash your hands when you are finished with the activity.

 Plant Safety Handle plants only as directed by your teacher. If you are allergic to certain plants, tell your teacher; do not do an activity involving those plants. Avoid touching harmful plants such as poison ivy. Wash your hands when you are finished with the activity.

 Electric Shock To avoid electric shock, never use electrical equipment around water, when the equipment is wet, or when your hands are wet. Be sure cords are untangled and cannot trip anyone. Unplug equipment not in use.

 Physical Safety When an experiment involves physical activity, avoid injuring yourself or others. Alert your teacher if there is any reason you should not participate.

 Disposal Dispose of chemicals and other laboratory materials safely. Follow the instructions from your teacher.

 Hand Washing Wash your hands thoroughly when finished with an activity. Use soap and warm water. Rinse well.

 General Safety Awareness When this symbol appears, follow the instructions provided. When you are asked to develop your own procedure in a lab, have your teacher approve your plan.

APPENDIX B

Using a Laboratory Balance

The laboratory balance is an important tool in scientific investigations. Different kinds of balances are used in the laboratory to determine the masses and weights of objects. You can use a triple-beam balance to determine the masses of materials that you study or experiment with in the laboratory. An electronic balance, unlike a triple-beam balance, is used to measure the weights of materials.

The triple-beam balance that you may use in your science class is probably similar to the balance depicted in this Appendix. To use the balance properly, you should learn the name, location, and function of each part of the balance.

Triple-Beam Balance

The triple-beam balance is a single-pan balance with three beams calibrated in grams. The back, or 100-gram, beam is divided into ten units of 10 grams each. The middle, or 500-gram, beam is divided into five units of 100 grams each. The front, or 10-gram, beam is divided into ten units of 1 gram each. Each gram on the front beam is further divided into units of 0.1 gram.

Apply Concepts What is the greatest mass you could find with the triple-beam balance in the picture?

....

Calculate What is the mass of the apple in the picture?

....

The following procedure can be used to find the mass of an object with a triple-beam balance:

1. Place the object on the pan.
2. Move the rider on the middle beam notch by notch until the horizontal pointer on the right drops below zero. Move the rider back one notch.
3. Move the rider on the back beam notch by notch until the pointer again drops below zero. Move the rider back one notch.
4. Slowly slide the rider along the front beam until the pointer stops at the zero point.
5. The mass of the object is equal to the sum of the readings on the three beams.

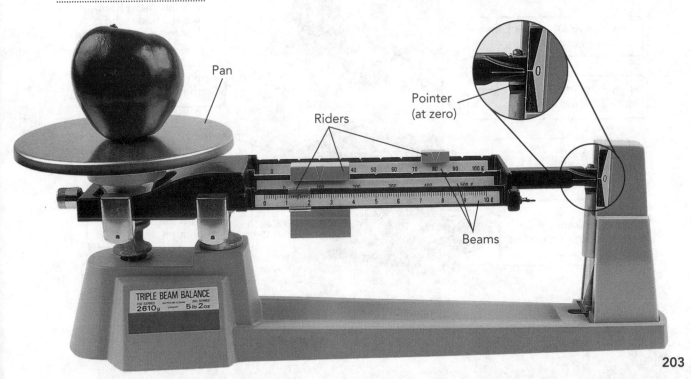

Pan · Riders · Pointer (at zero) · Beams

Using a Microscope

The microscope is an essential tool in the study of life science. It allows you to see things that are too small to be seen with the unaided eye.

You will probably use a compound microscope like the one you see here. The compound microscope has more than one lens that magnifies the object you view.

Typically, a compound microscope has one lens in the eyepiece (the part you look through). The eyepiece lens usually magnifies 10×. Any object you view through this lens will appear 10 times larger than it is.

A compound microscope may contain two or three other lenses called objective lenses. They are called the low-power and high-power objective lenses. The low-power objective lens usually magnifies 10×. The high-power objective lenses usually magnify 40× and 100×.

To calculate the total magnification with which you are viewing an object, multiply the magnification of the eyepiece lens by the magnification of the objective lens you are using. For example, the eyepiece's magnification of 10× multiplied by the low-power objective's magnification of 10× equals a total magnification of 100×.

Use the photo of the compound microscope to become familiar with the parts of the microscope and their functions.

The Parts of a Microscope

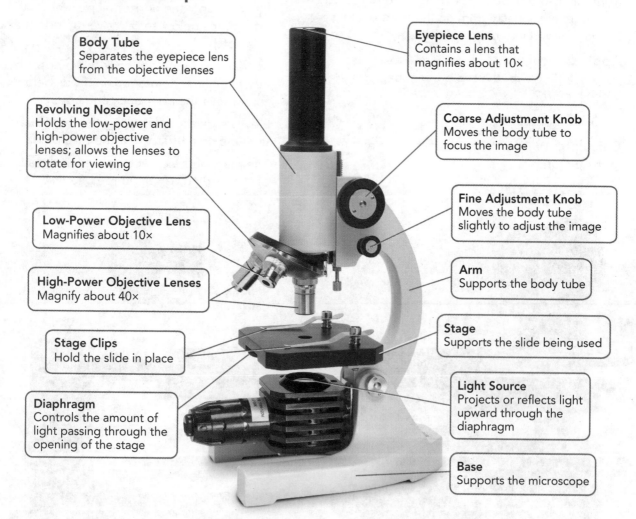

Body Tube
Separates the eyepiece lens from the objective lenses

Revolving Nosepiece
Holds the low-power and high-power objective lenses; allows the lenses to rotate for viewing

Low-Power Objective Lens
Magnifies about 10×

High-Power Objective Lenses
Magnify about 40×

Stage Clips
Hold the slide in place

Diaphragm
Controls the amount of light passing through the opening of the stage

Eyepiece Lens
Contains a lens that magnifies about 10×

Coarse Adjustment Knob
Moves the body tube to focus the image

Fine Adjustment Knob
Moves the body tube slightly to adjust the image

Arm
Supports the body tube

Stage
Supports the slide being used

Light Source
Projects or reflects light upward through the diaphragm

Base
Supports the microscope

Using the Microscope

Use the following procedures when you are working with a microscope.

1. To carry the microscope, grasp the microscope's arm with one hand. Place your other hand under the base.

2. Place the microscope on a table with the arm toward you.

3. Turn the coarse adjustment knob to raise the body tube.

4. Revolve the nosepiece until the low-power objective lens clicks into place.

5. Adjust the diaphragm. While looking through the eyepiece, adjust the mirror until you see a bright white circle of light. **CAUTION:** Never use direct sunlight as a light source.

6. Place a slide on the stage. Center the specimen over the opening on the stage. Use the stage clips to hold the slide in place. **CAUTION:** Glass slides are fragile.

7. Look at the stage from the side. Carefully turn the coarse adjustment knob to lower the body tube until the low-power objective almost touches the slide.

8. Looking through the eyepiece, very slowly turn the coarse adjustment knob until the specimen comes into focus.

9. To switch to the high-power objective lens, look at the microscope from the side. Carefully revolve the nosepiece until the high-power objective lens clicks into place. Make sure the lens does not hit the slide.

10. Looking through the eyepiece, turn the fine adjustment knob until the specimen comes into focus.

Making a Wet-Mount Slide

Use the following procedures to make a wet-mount slide of a specimen.

1. Obtain a clean microscope slide and a coverslip. **CAUTION:** Glass slides and coverslips are fragile.

2. Place the specimen on the center of the slide. The specimen must be thin enough for light to pass through it.

3. Using a plastic dropper, place a drop of water on the specimen.

4. Gently place one edge of the coverslip against the slide so that it touches the edge of the water drop at a 45° angle. Slowly lower the coverslip over the specimen. If you see air bubbles trapped beneath the coverslip, tap the coverslip gently with the eraser end of a pencil.

5. Remove any excess water at the edge of the coverslip with a paper towel.

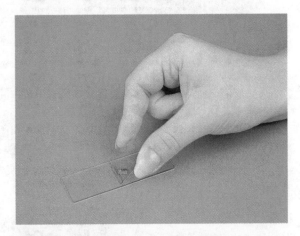

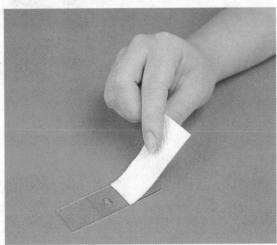

Periodic Table of Elements

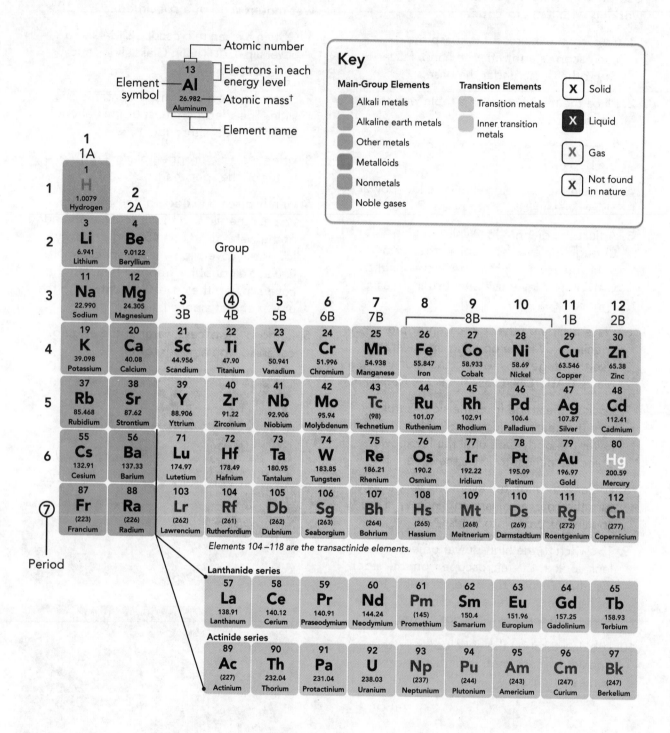

Elements 104–118 are the transactinide elements.

†The atomic masses in parentheses are the mass numbers of the longest-lived isotope of elements for which a standard atomic mass cannot be defined.

18 8A
2 **He** 4.0026 Helium

13 3A	14 4A	15 5A	16 6A	17 7A	
5 **B** 10.81 Boron	6 **C** 12.011 Carbon	7 **N** 14.007 Nitrogen	8 **O** 15.999 Oxygen	9 **F** 18.998 Fluorine	10 **Ne** 20.179 Neon
13 **Al** 26.982 Aluminum	14 **Si** 28.086 Silicon	15 **P** 30.974 Phosphorus	16 **S** 32.06 Sulfur	17 **Cl** 35.453 Chlorine	18 **Ar** 39.948 Argon
31 **Ga** 69.72 Gallium	32 **Ge** 72.59 Germanium	33 **As** 74.922 Arsenic	34 **Se** 78.96 Selenium	35 **Br** 79.904 Bromine	36 **Kr** 83.80 Krypton
49 **In** 114.82 Indium	50 **Sn** 118.69 Tin	51 **Sb** 121.75 Antimony	52 **Te** 127.60 Tellurium	53 **I** 126.90 Iodine	54 **Xe** 131.30 Xenon
81 **Tl** 204.37 Thallium	82 **Pb** 207.2 Lead	83 **Bi** 208.98 Bismuth	84 **Po** (209) Polonium	85 **At** (210) Astatine	86 **Rn** (222) Radon
113 **Nh** (284) Nihonium	114 **Fl** (289) Flerovium	115 **Mc** (288) Moscovium	116 **Lv** (292) Livermorium	117 **Ts** (294) Tennessine	118 **Og** (294) Oganesson

66 **Dy** 162.50 Dysprosium	67 **Ho** 164.93 Holmium	68 **Er** 167.26 Erbium	69 **Tm** 168.93 Thulium	70 **Yb** 173.04 Ytterbium
98 **Cf** (251) Californium	99 **Es** (252) Einsteinium	100 **Fm** (257) Fermium	101 **Md** (258) Mendelevium	102 **No** (259) Nobelium

GLOSSARY

A

absolute age The age of a rock given as the number of years since the rock formed. (155)

amphibian A vertebrate whose body temperature is determined by the temperature of its environment, and that lives its early life in water and its adult life on land. (174)

aquifer An underground layer of rock or sediment that holds water. (30)

atmosphere The relatively thin layer of gases that form Earth's outermost layer. (6)

B

biosphere The parts of Earth that contain living organisms. (6)

C

coastline A line that forms the boundary between the land and the ocean or a lake. (17)

compression Stress that squeezes rock until it folds or breaks. (121)

condensation The change in state from a gas to a liquid. (26)

convergent boundary A plate boundary where two plates move toward each other. (113)

crust The layer of rock that forms Earth's outer surface. (52)

cryosphere The portion of the hydrosphere that is frozen, including all the ice and snow on land, plus sea and lake ice. (6)

crystal A solid in which the atoms are arranged in a pattern that repeats again and again. (61)

crystallization The process by which atoms are arranged to form a material with a crystal structure. (65)

D

delta A landform made of sediment that is deposited where a river flows into an ocean or lake. (17)

divergent boundary A plate boundary where two plates move away from each other. (113)

dormant Term used to describe a volcano that is not currently acrtive but able to become active in the future. (138)

dune A hill of sand piled up by the wind. (17)

E

earthquake The shaking that results from the movement of rock beneath Earth's surface. (125)

energy The ability to do work or cause change. (7)

era One of the three long units of geologic time between the Precambrian and the present. (168)

evaporation The process by which molecules at the surface of a liquid absorb enough energy to change to a gas. (25)

extinct 1. Term used to describe a volcano that is no longer active and unlikely to erupt again. 2. Term used to refer to a group of related organisms that has died out and has no living members. (138)

F

fault A break in Earth's crust along which rocks move. (122)

fossil The preserved remains or traces of an organism that lived in the past. (157)

G

geologic time scale A record of the geologic events and life forms in Earth's history. (165)

geosphere The densest parts of Earth that include the crust, mantle, and core. (6)

H

hot spot An area where magma from deep within the mantle melts through the crust above it. (135)

hydrosphere The portion of Earth that consists of water in any of its forms, including oceans, glaciers, rivers, lakes, groundwater and water vapor. (6)

I

igneous rock A type of rock that forms from the cooling of molten rock at or below the surface. (73)

inner core A dense sphere of solid iron and nickel at the center of Earth. (54)

invertebrate An animal without a backbone. (173)

L

landform A feature on the surface of Earth, such as a coastline, dune, or mountain. (13)

lava Liquid magma that reaches the surface. (133)

law of superposition The geologic principle that states that in horizontal layers of sedimentary rock, each layer is older than the layer above it and younger than the layer below it. (156)

M

magma A molten mixture of rock-forming substances, gases, and water from the mantle. (133)

magnitude The measurement of an earthquake's strength based on seismic waves and movement along faults. (127)

mammal A vertebrate whose body temperature is regulated by its internal heat, and that has skin covered with hair or fur and glands that produce milk to feed its young. (176)

mantle The layer of hot, solid material between Earth's crust and core. (53)

mass extinction When many types of living things become extinct at the same time. (175)

metamorphic rock A type of rock that forms from an existing rock that is changed by heat, pressure, or chemical reactions. (75)

mid-ocean ridge An undersea mountain chain where new ocean floor is produced; a divergent plate boundary under the ocean. (102)

mineral A naturally occurring solid that can form by inorganic processes and that has a crystal structure and a definite chemical composition. (61)

mountain A landform with high elevation and high relief. (16)

O

ocean trench An undersea valley that represents one of the deepest parts of the ocean. (104)

outer core A layer of molten iron and nickel that surrounds the inner core of Earth. (54)

period One of the units of geologic time into which geologists divide eras. (168)

P

precipitation Any form of water that falls from clouds and reaches Earth's surface as rain, snow, sleet, or hail. (26)

R

radioactive dating The process of determining the age of an object using the half-life of one or more radioactive isotopes. (160)

radioactive decay The process in which the nuclei of radioactive elements break down, releasing fastmoving particles and energy. (159)

relative age The age of a rock compared to the ages of other rocks. (155)

reptile A vertebrate whose temperature is determined by the temperature of its environment, that has lungs and scaly skin, and that lays eggs on land. (174)

river A natural stream of water that flows into another body of water, such as an ocean, lake, or another river. (17)

rock cycle A series of processes on the surface and inside Earth that slowly changes rocks from one kind to another. (79)

S

sea-floor spreading The process by which molten material adds new oceanic crust to the ocean floor. (103)

sediment Small, solid pieces of material that come from rocks or the remains of organisms; earth materials deposited by erosion. (74)

sedimentary rock A type of rock that forms when particles from other rocks or the remains of plants and animals are pressed and cemented together. (74)

seismic wave Vibrations that travel through Earth carrying the energy released during an earthquake. (50)

shearing Stress that pushes masses of rock in opposite directions, in a sideways movement. (121)

stress A force that acts on rock to change its shape or volume. (121)"

subduction The process by which oceanic crust sinks beneath a deep-ocean trench and back into the mantle at a convergent plate boundary. (104)

surveying A process in which mapmakers determine distances and elevations using instruments and the principles of geometry. (18)

T

tension Stress that stretches rock so that it becomes thinner in the middle. (121)

topography The shape of the land determined by elevation, relief, and landforms. (13)

transform boundary A plate boundary where two plates move past each other in opposite directions. (113)

transpiration The process by which water is lost through a plant's leaves. (25)

tsunami A giant wave usually caused by an earthquake beneath the ocean floor. (129)

U

unconformity A gap in the geologic record that shows where rock layers have been lost due to erosion. (158)

V

vertebrate An animal with a backbone. (174)

volcano A weak spot in the crust where magma has come to the surface. (133)

W

water cycle The continual movement of water among Earth's atmosphere, oceans, and land surface through evaporation, condensation, and precipitation. (25)

watershed The land area that supplies water to a river system. (28)

well A hole sunk into the ground to reach a supply of water. (30)

INDEX

Page numbers for key terms are printed in boldface type.

INDEX Page numbers for key terms are printed in boldface type.

CREDITS

Photographs
Photo locators denoted as follows: Top (T), Center (C), Bottom (B), Left (L), Right (R), Background (Bkgd)

Covers
Front Cover: Lightphoto/iStock/Getty Images
Back Cover: LHF Graphics/Shutterstock

Front Matter
iv: Clari Massimiliano/Shutterstock; vi: Mark Whitt Photography/Getty Images; vii: Demerzel21/Fotolia; viii: AFP/Getty Images; ix: Sinclair Stammers/Science Photo Library/Getty Images; x: Brian J. Skerry/National Geographic/Getty Images; xi: Gary Meszaros/Science Source/Getty Images.

Topic 1
xii: Mark Whitt Photography/Getty Images002 Bkgrd: 123RF; 002 TR: Tfoxfoto/Getty Images; 004: Samuel Borges/Alamy Stock Photo; 006 BL: Marco Regalia/Alamy Stock Photo; 006 CL: Dorota Wasik/EyeEm/Getty; 007 BR: Panther Media GmbH/Alamy Stock Photo; 007 CR: Marco Regalia/Alamy Stock Photo; 011: Seafarer/Shuttesrstock; 014: David Pearson/Alamy Stock Photo; 015: Stocktrek Images, Inc./Alamy Stock Photo; 018: Charles Gurche/Danita Delimont/Alamy Stock Photo; 020 B: UniversalImagesGroup/Contributor/Getty Images; 020 T: Tetra Images/Alamy Stock Photo; 023 BCR: Songquan Deng/Shutterstock; 023 CR: Everett Collection/Shutterstock; 024: Paul Prescott/Shutterstock; 028: Clint Farlinger/Alamy Stock Photo; 029 CR: Aurora Photos/Alamy Stock Photo; 029 TR: ImageBROKER/Alamy Stock Photo; 034: NASA; 037: Westend61/Getty Images; 038: NASA; 040: Sergio Azenha/Alamy Stock Photo; 041: BW Folsom/Shutterstock;

Topic 2
044: Demerzel21/Fotolia; 046: John Bryson/The LIFE Images Collection/Getty Images; 048: Wead/Shutterstock; 049: John Cancalosi/Getty Images; 057: Paul Silverman/Fundamental Photographs; 059: AOES Medialab/ESA; 069 B: Per Anders Pettersson/Getty Images; 069 TR: Eric Baccega/AGE Fotostock/Alamy Stock Photo; 070: Brian Jannsen/Alamy Stock Photo; 076: Wead/Shutterstock; 078: Michael Routh/Alamy Stock Photo; 080: Kmartin457/Getty Images; 081 C: Mark Yarchoan/Shutterstock; 081 CL: Joel Arem/Science Source; 081 CR: 123RF; 081 TCL: Tom Holt/Alamy Stock Photo; 081 TCR: Trevor Clifford/Pearson Education Ltd; 084 Bkgrd: Brandon B/Shutterstock; 084 CL: Universal Images Group North America LLC/Alamy Stock Photo; 090: Jon Bilous/Shutterstock; 091 B: MM Studio/Fotolia; 091 CR: Pavlo Burdyak/123RF; 091: I m a g e/Shutterstock;

Topic 3
094: AFP/Getty Images; 096: Christopher Boswell/Shutterstock; 103 TL: Mr. Elliot Lim and Mr. Jesse Varner, CIRES & NOAA/NCEI; 103 TR: OAR/National Undersea Research Program/NOAA; 107: Sueddeutsche Zeitung Photo/Alamy Stock Photo; 108: MarkushaBLR/Fotolia; 114: Wildestanimal/Moment Open/Getty Images; 115 B: Room27/Shutterstock; 115 CR: David Burton/Alamy Stock Photo; 118: Travel Pictures/Alamy Stock Photo; 120: The Asahi Shimbun/Getty Images; 129: JIJI PRESS/AFP/Getty Images; 131: Epa European Pressphoto Agency b.v./Alamy Stock Photo; 132:

Pall Gudonsson/Getty Images; 138 TL: Siim Sepp/Alamy Stock Photo; 138 TR: Sandatlas/Shutterstock; 139: Hulton Archive/Getty Images; 140 BR: Rosa Irene Betancourt 3/Alamy Stock Photo; 140 TL: Janet Babb/Hawaiian Volcano Observatory/U.S. Geological Survey,; 147: Space_Expert/Fotolia;

Topic 4
150: Sinclair Stammers/Science Photo Library/Getty Images; 152: James L. Amos/Science Source; 154: Jim in SC/Shutterstock; 156 BL: Carol Dembinsky/Dembinsky Photo Associates/Alamy Stock Photo; 156 BR: Chris Curtis/Shutterstock; 162: Greenfire/Fotolia; 164: Mark Godden/Shutterstock; 166 BL: Chase Studio/Science Source; 166 BR: Ralf Juergen Kraft/Shutterstock; 167 BR: Catmando/Shutterstock; 167 TC: DEA/G. CIGOLINI/Getty Images; 167 TL: Jean Philippe Delobelle/Alamy Stock Photo; 168: Biophoto Associates/Science Source; 171: James King Holmes/Science Source; 172: Laurie O'Keefe/Science Source; 174: MarcelClemens/Shutterstock; 175 TL: John Cancalosi/Alamy Stock Photo; 175 TR: Sabena Jane Blackbird/Alamy Stock Photo; 176 BR: Herschel Hoffmeyer/Shutterstock; 176 BR: Stocktrek Images, Inc./Alamy Stock Photo; 178 B: The Natural History Museum/The Image Works; 178 TL: Jerry Young/Dorling Kindersley; 179 BC: Andreas Meyer/123RF; 179 C: Bedrock Studios/Dorling Kindersley; 179 TC: Chase Studio/Science Source; 181 B: Sean Pavone/Alamy Stock Photo; 181 TR: Alan Novelli/Getty Images; 186: Jonathan Blair/Getty Images; 187: Adwo/Shutterstock;

End Matter
190 BCL: Philippe Plailly & Elisabeth Daynes/Science Source; 190 BL: EHStockphoto/Shutterstock; 190 TCL: Cyndi Monaghan/Getty Images; 190 TL: Javier Larrea/AGE Fotostock; 191: WaterFrame/Alamy Stock Photo; 192: Africa Studio/Shutterstock; 193: Jeff Rotman/Alamy Stock Photo; 194: Grant Faint/Getty Images; 195: Ross Armstrong/Alamy Stock Photo; 196: Geoz/Alamy Stock Photo; 199: Martin Shields/Alamy Stock Photo; 200: Nicola Tree/Getty Images; 201: Regan Geeseman/NASA; 203 : Pearson Education Ltd.; 204: Pearson Education Ltd.; 205 BR: Pearson Education Ltd.; 205 TR: Pearson Education Ltd.

Program graphics: ArtMari/Shutterstock; BeatWalk/Shutterstock; Irmun/Shutterstock; LHF Graphics/Shutterstock; Multigon/Shutterstock; Nikolaeva/Shutterstock; silm/Shutterstock; Undrey/Shutterstock

Take Notes

Use this space for recording notes and sketching out ideas.

Take Notes

Use this space for recording notes and sketching out ideas.